Brookings Occasional Papers

Assessing the Adversary

Estimates by the Eisenhower Administration
of
Soviet Intentions and Capabilities

RAYMOND L. GARTHOFF

THE BROOKINGS INSTITUTION

Washington, D.C.

Brookings Occasional Papers

THE BROOKINGS INSTITUTION is a private nonprofit organization devoted to research, education, and publication on important issues of domestic and foreign policy. Its principal purpose is to bring knowledge to bear on the major policy problems facing the American people.

On occasion Brookings staff members produce research papers that warrant immediate circulation as contributions to the public debate on current issues of national importance. Because of the speed of their production, these Occasional Papers are not subjected to all of the formal review procedures established for the Institution's research publications, and they may be revised at a later date. As in all Brookings publications, the judgments, conclusions, and recommendations presented in the Papers are solely those of the authors and should not be attributed to the trustees, officers, or other staff members of the Institution.

Acknowledgements

This paper was originally prepared for a conference on the Eisenhower legacy in world affairs held in Moscow in November 1990, bringing together American and Soviet scholars of and veteran participants in U.S. and Soviet policymaking in the years of the administration of President Dwight D. Eisenhower. An abbreviated version will appear in proceedings of that conference.

As required, owing to the author's service in the Central Intelligence Agency in the years 1957–61, the manuscript was reviewed by that agency to assure that it did not inadvertently disclose any currently security-classified information and has been cleared for publication.

The author wishes to express appreciation to Venka Macintyre for editing assistance, to Louise Skillings for preparing the manuscript for publication, and to Susan F. Woollen for typesetting the paper.

Brookings gratefully acknowledges financial support for this project by the John D. and Catherine T. MacArthur Foundation and the Carnegie Corporation of New York.

Raymond L. Garthoff is a senior fellow in the Brookings Foreign Policy Studies program.

Part 1
The Post-Stalin Years (1953–56)

The fundamental question underlying one government's assessments of another, particularly an adversary, pertains to its intentions. If it is perceived to be an adversary, a competitor for political influence, and a potential military opponent, that question has already been answered, at least in part. Other questions concerning intention nonetheless remain important: are the adversary's aims limited or unlimited; are its designs and plans for expanding its influence set or flexible, limited or unconstrained; do its policies pose a direct or indirect challenge; do its predicted actions create a need for countermeasures, including measures to head off threats before they materialize? Clearly, such questions must embrace capabilities as well as intentions, inasmuch as policies and actions are necessarily based on relative capabilities (or, to be more precise, on judgments about relative capabilities). What are its potentialities, particularly to cause one harm, and what are its vulnerabilities to one's own actions?

Any leadership approaches such questions from the standpoint of its situation at a given point in time, but also as part of a continuum heavily influenced by past assessments. There is, in practice, never a tabula rasa. Certainly, there was none for the incoming Eisenhower administration. While stressing (and exaggerating) differences with its predecessor over policy, it shared fully the American consensus of the late 1940s and early 1950s that the Soviet Union had expansionist designs. Soviet aims and policies were seen as based on ingrained ideological hostility and a pursuit of world domination. Although containment was criticized both as too weak a response (and yet also as too debilitating), the perceived challenge was essentially the same as it had been for the Truman administration ever since 1946–47. General assessments of Soviet objectives, and also estimates of Soviet positions on specific issues, were formulated in a context in which basic judgments had already been made and were taken for granted.

Assessments of an adversary include formal statements and estimates made by the president and his top security policy advisers, in particular National Security Council (NSC) policy guidance, and those made by the intelligence agencies, in

1

particular coordinated National Intelligence Estimates (NIEs) and Special National Intelligence Estimates (SNIEs).[1] Assessments of an adversary also include a full panoply of formal, informal, and sometimes implicit and even unconscious evaluations and judgments by various individuals and agencies of government. The president, the secretary of state, and other key advisers to the president (in recent years assistants to the president for national security affairs such as McGeorge Bundy, Walt Rostow, Henry Kissinger, and Zbigniew Brzezinski, but far less so in the Eisenhower years), key State Department advisers and Soviet affairs experts, and others can play important roles. Less directly, and only partly subject to administration influence and leadership, the sentiments of the Congress and the public are ultimately, and on occasion directly, important.

In the Eisenhower administration, the key "assessor" was clearly President Dwight D. Eisenhower himself. Second in importance (until his death in 1959) was Secretary of State John Foster Dulles. Others whose views of Soviet policy mattered included a number of White House advisers, such as C. D. Jackson (and his successor Nelson A. Rockefeller), occupying a new position as special assistant to the president for cold war planning and "the president's representative" on the Operations Coordinating Board (OCB), formerly the Truman administration's Psychological Strategy Board (PSB), which was renamed when it was given a broader mandate. In the State Department, the head of the Policy Planning Staff, Robert Bowie (who succeeded Paul Nitze in the post a few months after the change of administration), played a role, along with several European and Soviet affairs experts. From 1953 to 1957 Charles (Chip) Bohlen, and from 1957 to 1961 Llewellyn (Tommy) Thompson, served as ambassador in Moscow.[2] Allen Dulles,

---

1. The preparation of coordinated National Intelligence Estimates was instituted in 1950 in the wake of the failure of the several intelligence agencies to anticipate the launching of the Korean War. It continues to this day, although the Office of National Estimates (ONE), with a senior board and expert staff, was replaced in 1973 by a panel (later loosely joined as a council) of senior national intelligence officers (NIOs). During the Eisenhower years, estimates were drafted by the ONE, using at their discretion contributions from other agencies, and all intelligence agencies (together constituting the intelligence community) participated in refining and coordinating the final product, National Intelligence Estimates, issued by the director of Central Intelligence and concurred in by the Intelligence Advisory Committee (in 1958 renamed the United States Intelligence Board). The Soviet Union, in contrast, to this day does not have a system of providing coordinated national intelligence estimates.

2. The most prominent Soviet affairs expert, Ambassador George Kennan, was forced to retire by Secretary John F. Dulles, without even a letter of appreciation from him. Allen Dulles, however, kept in contact with Kennan and used him as an expert consultant to the CIA in its national intelligence estimates. Even though Bohlen was President Eisenhower's personal choice for Moscow, the new administration was tepid in his defense when his nomination faced a McCarthyite challenge in Senate hearings, and in 1957 Bohlen himself was "exiled" as ambassador to the Philippines.

brother of the secretary of state, was named director of Central Intelligence and of the Central Intelligence Agency (CIA), which he headed during what was probably its heyday of prestige from 1953 into 1961.

President Eisenhower, in his memoirs, spoke with respect of the intelligence estimates, which, he said, "we studied constantly with experts in many fields."[3] In practice, most intelligence estimates of Soviet objectives and policy exerted such influence as they had through national security policy papers. Estimates in crises or on particular issues had varying influence, some significant and others not.

The Eisenhower administration continued the practice of its predecessor in formulating basic national security policy in a formal document, along the lines first laid down in 1948, but most fully in 1950 in NSC 68, "United States Objectives and Programs for National Security."[4] In fact, two editions of "Basic National Security Policy" (BNSP) were prepared in 1953, and one each year thereafter through the eight years of the Eisenhower administration.[5] The first prepared by the Eisenhower administration was issued as NSC 153/1 in June 1953.[6] A revised BNSP, with new guidelines on military policy and on "massive retaliation" but no real change in assessment of the adversary, was issued as NSC 162/2 in October 1953.[7] Before considering the assessments reflected in these and related policy papers, several developments in the overall situation call for comment.

It is also necessary to bear in mind that the present discussion is not an analysis of policymaking beyond a consideration of the assessment of the adversary, and not a review of policy implementation or of the course of relations between the two countries. Thus, for example, disarmament talks or other negotiations are not treated except in terms of the role of assessment of Soviet leaders and policies in setting U.S. policy objectives and directives.

Part 1 of this discussion examines assessments in the first Eisenhower administration of Soviet intentions and capabilities—principally, vulnerabilities—in

3. Dwight D. Eisenhower, *The White House Years: Mandate for Change, 1953–1956* (Doubleday, 1963), p. 149. (Hereafter *Mandate for Change*.)

4. See *Foreign Relations of the United States 1948* (U.S. Department of State, 1976), vol. 1, pt. 2, pp. 662–69 (hereafter *FRUS* [year]); and *FRUS 1950* (1977), vol. 1, pp. 234–92.

5. President John F. Kennedy decided to discontinue the preparation of such BNSP guidance because he believed such a basic document would unduly constrain flexibility in meeting policy issues as they arose.

6. See *FRUS 1952–1954* (1984), vol. 2, pp. 378–86. The outgoing administration, on its last day in office, had updated its own policy paper as a legacy, NSC 141; see ibid., pp. 209–22.

7. See ibid., pp. 489–534, 565–67, 577–79.

a time of clear American superiority and initiative. Part 2 deals with the second Eisenhower administration, which early on had to shift its focus to Soviet capabilities and intentions in a time of perceived Soviet advance and declining American advantage, the post-Sputnik years of the missile gap, and Soviet pressures on West Berlin.

Within a span of less than forty-five days during the first quarter of 1953, important changes in leadership took place both in Moscow and in Washington, the first such changes since the cold war had begun. The change was to prove more fundamental in the Soviet case, with the passing of Stalin from the scene, and was less than anticipated in the U.S. case (given the rhetoric of the electoral campaign), but in neither country were the policy consequences evident for some time.

Changes in Soviet foreign policy, when they did come, were also important—but this, too, was not evident. One of the key questions for assessors in the Eisenhower administration was whether, how much, how enduring, and with what consequences for U.S. policy were changes in Soviet objectives and policy significant. Only three months after the change in Soviet leadership, the first Eisenhower BNSP clearly reflected the new intelligence and policy assessment: "Although the USSR has recently assumed a more conciliatory posture in its dealings with the West, there is no basis for concluding that the fundamental hostility of the Kremlin toward the West has abated, that the ultimate objectives of the Soviet rulers have changed, or that the menace of communism to the free world has diminished."[8] This judgment remained essentially unchanged throughout the Eisenhower administration.[9]

President Eisenhower expressed his own assessment of the driving motivation of all Soviet leaders in a later evaluation of Nikita Khrushchev, whom he found to be "blinded by his dedication to the Marxist theory of world revolution and Communist domination."[10] Incomplete as that evaluation may be, Eisenhower felt it was confirmed by Khrushchev's frequent boasts about the advance of communism and the ominous-sounding prognostication that "we will bury you."

8. NSC 153/1, June 10, 1953, in ibid., p. 380; see also NIE 99, "Estimate of the World Situation through 1955," October 23, 1953, ibid., p. 551.

9. For example, the latest annual NIE on Soviet policy that has been declassified (NIE 11-4-57, *Main Trends in Soviet Capabilities and Policies, 1957–1962*, November 12, 1957), while crediting Khrushchev with "flexibility and pragmatism," contended that "none of the changes in Soviet policy suggests any alteration in basic aims or in the concept of an irreconcilable conflict between the Communist and non-Communist worlds" (para. 1, p. 1); see *FRUS 1955–1957* (1990), vol. 19, p. 665.

10. Eisenhower, *Mandate for Change*, p. 522. President Eisenhower himself, like President Harry S. Truman, notwithstanding the contrary view of all the professional experts, believed—as he

Thus, from the outset, the Eisenhower administration saw the Soviet Union as an adversary whose basic hostility and ultimate expansionist objectives were unchangeable. Changes of policy and action were considered shifts in "tactics" and "posture," not in strategy or aims.

President Eisenhower's inaugural address had stated his general policy objectives, but it was not precise about his administration's policy toward the Soviet Union. In a press conference in February, the president had indicated a general readiness to meet anyone anywhere if such a meeting would be useful.[11] But the first priming event that required a more concrete definition of policy was the death of Stalin on March 5, 1953.

Truman's Psychological Strategy Board had been studying possibilities for U.S. action and preparing for the death of Stalin for over a year, but there was no agreed "plan," as Eisenhower noted with some annoyance. The analysts examining the subject had observed that although changes after Stalin might (as expected) be for the better, they might instead be for the worse—at the extreme "possibly even general war"—or a general collapse.[12] Fortunately, no precipitous action was taken by the United States.[13] The administration watched closely the emergence of the new leadership, but it believed that all Soviet leaders pursued the same ultimate aims.

A Special National Intelligence Estimate on March 12 predicted that at least for the near term "the new Soviet leadership will almost certainly pursue the foreign and domestic policies established during recent years. In particular it will

---

said in an NSC meeting on March 11, 1953—that the Soviet Union had taken the path of the cold war only because "Stalin had had to come to terms with the other members of the Kremlin circle," that if Stalin had had his own way after the war, "Russia would have sought more peaceful and normal relations with the rest of the world." None of his advisers supported this comment (nor, however, did any directly contradict it). See *FRUS 1952–1954* (1988), vol. 8, p. 1118.

Secretary of State Dulles, who after 1946 had steeped himself in Stalin's *Problems of Leninism* and other communist ideological treatises, prided himself on his expertise in understanding the Soviet/communist mind. He was confident that communist leaders of the Soviet Union were all of a predetermined mold, with room for variation in policy tactics but not in ultimate aims. Son of a Presbyterian minister, he was familiar with a doctrine of predestination. He often spoke of the atheistic communist "faith."

11. Eisenhower, *Mandate for Change*, p. 143.

12. PSB D-24, "Program of Psychological Preparation for Stalin's Passing," *FRUS 1952–1954*, vol. 8, pp. 1059–60. See also a similar intelligence caution, in SE-39, "Probable Consequences of the Death of Stalin and of the Elevation of Malenkov to Leadership in the USSR," March 10, 1953, in ibid., pp. 1125–29. ("Special Estimates," SE series, was the forerunner of SNIEs.)

13. The U.S. Air Force Psychological Warfare Division (PWD) had prepared Russian-language propaganda leaflets and reportedly had even begun to load them on bombers in anticipation of approval to drop them over the Soviet Union, before being estopped. Information from my conversations with the chief of the PWD at that time.

probably continue to emphasize unremitting hostility to the West . . . and the increase of Bloc military power."[14] A new appraisal a little over a month later recognized that there had been "developments within the USSR which may prove to be of profound significance for Soviet foreign policy," including a possible struggle for power within the leadership. But it also voiced what was to become the standard litany: "There is no basis for concluding that the fundamental hostility of the Kremlin toward the West has abated, that the ultimate objectives of the Soviet rulers have changed, or that the menace of Communism to the free world has diminished."[15] This was also essentially the view of Ambassador Bohlen in Moscow, although he urged Washington—in terms discordant with the dominant view there—not to attempt "for the sake of superficial and temporary propaganda gains to 'put the Soviet Government on the spot,'" but rather to "consider every possibility of inducing or forcing the new leadership to commit itself more deeply to the line advanced since the death of Stalin."[16]

President Eisenhower decided to take the initiative in a speech delivered on April 16, 1953.[17] He proposed that the new Soviet leadership seize the "chance for peace" and join in the opportunity to help "turn back the black tide of events." He called for deeds, not rhetoric—specifically, a truce in Korea, an Austrian treaty and neutralization, the release of World War II prisoners of war, and especially steps toward disarmament to relieve mankind of the burden of the arms race. There was no hint of the electoral campaign slogan in which he had promised to press for the liberation of the satellite states of Eastern Europe (except for a challenging rhetorical question asking whether the Soviet Union was prepared to allow the nations of Eastern Europe a free choice of governments).[18]

President Eisenhower did not, however, endorse Prime Minister Winston Churchill's public call on May 11 for a summit. He had even dropped from his own speech any reference to his February statement of readiness to meet the Soviet leader. Moreover, he did not later take into account that virtually all of

14. See SE-39, in Frus 1952–1954, vol. 8, p. 1127. SE-39 was, however, a good overall estimate of the initial consequences in the Soviet Union of Stalin's demise.

15. See SE-42, "Current Communist Tactics," April 24, 1953, in ibid., pp. 1160–62, quotation p. 1162.

16. Ambassador Bohlen, Embassy Moscow cable 1518 to the Secretary of State, April 24, 1953, in ibid., pp. 1156–59, quotation p. 1159. See also Bohlen's subsequent messages of July 7 and 9, 1953, ibid., pp. 1193–96, 1205–06.

17. See Eisenhower, *Mandate for Change*, pp. 145–48.

18. See "The Chance for Peace: Address by the President," *Department of State Bulletin*, vol. 27 (April 27, 1953), pp. 599–603, quotations pp. 603, 602. (Hereafter *DOSB*.)

his litmus test proposals had been met.[19] He had said, for example, that "even a few such clear and specific acts" as the Austrian treaty would be "impressive signs of sincere intent." Yet he failed to acknowledge that within two years the Austrian treaty and the Korean armistice had been signed, the World War II POWs had been released, and the Soviet Union had even accepted the basic Western disarmament proposal—which the United States had walked away from.

The April 16 speech was a good one. I believe President Eisenhower hoped that it would encourage a favorable Soviet reaction. Nonetheless, the speech was originally designed, and later served, primarily to fortify the American stance rather than to induce Soviet change. It was seen primarily as an opportunity for effective political warfare against the Soviet Union rather than an opportunity for testing possible political accommodation by the new Soviet leadership. Its principal authors, Walt Rostow and C. D. Jackson (together with speechwriter Emmet J. Hughes), saw it as "the opening gun of the post-Stalin phase of the Cold War."[20]

Secretary Dulles, who had not been keen on the idea of the president's speech, followed it only two days later with an acerbic and challenging cold war speech.[21] Dulles's remarks brimmed with liberation rhetoric and set the president's own address not in the context of meeting change in the Soviet Union and what he disparagingly called Moscow's "peace defensive," but of reporting on the first ninety days of "the Eisenhower era," which he held had succeeded "the Stalin era," thus implying a shift from Soviet initiative in the world (also subtly downgrading President Truman) to American initiative.[22]

The president made a second major speech to the UN General Assembly in December 1953, again taking the propaganda initiative in his Atoms for Peace

19. Secretary Dulles had been responsible for introducing the litmus test list into the president's speech but was not inclined later to credit their fulfillment. On Dulles's role in inserting the tests in the speech, see Townsend Hoopes, *The Devil and John Foster Dulles* (Little, Brown, 1973), p. 172.

20. This felicitous phrase is that of Blanche Weiss Cook, *The Declassified Eisenhower: A Divided Legacy* (Doubleday, 1981), p. 179. For a comprehensive review of the origins of the speech by one of those directly involved, see W. W. Rostow, *Europe after Stalin: Eisenhower's Three Decisions of March 11, 1953* (University of Texas Press, 1982).

21. See Emmet John Hughes, *The Ordeal of Power* (Atheneum, 1963), p. 109.

22. "The First 90 Days: Address by Secretary Dulles," *DOSB*, vol. 27 (April 27, 1953), pp. 603–08, quotation pp. 607–08. Dulles had first contrasted the Stalin and succeeding Eisenhower eras on March 9. Dulles's speech was certainly an example of a more confrontational line toward the Soviet Union than the president had taken, and Dulles did tend to give somewhat more consistent emphasis to waging the cold war. It would, however, distort the record to conclude that there was a clear divide between a détente-minded president and a hard-line secretary of state, as some scholars have been inclined to do. See, for example, Robert A. Divine, *Eisenhower and the Cold War* (Oxford University Press, 1981), p. 106. For a useful recent set of essays based on the Dulles records, see Richard H. Immerman, ed., *John Foster Dulles and the Diplomacy of the Cold War* (Princeton University Press, 1990).

proposal. This proposal not only made a point of Soviet inferiority, but also took the negative aura off atomic energy by promoting nuclear disarmament coupled with the peaceful exploitation of atomic power. The reciprocal Soviet and U.S. conversion of some portion of their nuclear weapons arsenals could not have been accepted by Moscow. It was a propaganda gesture and an act of political warfare. As President Eisenhower stated in his memoirs, in defending the proposal against hard-line U.S. critics who feared that if accepted it would have jeopardized American nuclear strength, "Our technical experts assured me that even if Russia agreed to cooperate in such a plan . . . the United States could afford to reduce its atomic stockpile by two or three times the amount [of fissionable material] the Russians might contribute, and *still improve our relative [strategic] posture.*"[23] Small wonder the Soviet side rejected the proposal. But there is no indication that anyone in the administration was concerned about its impact on any *Soviet* assessment of *U.S.* intentions; the Soviet position was assumed in any case to be dedicated to a maximum contest short of war, with reciprocal hostility axiomatic.

In the summer of 1953, the administration conducted a major analytical exercise called Project Solarium. It focused on U.S.-Soviet relations, although it was concerned more with the optimum U.S. strategy for waging the cold war than with assessing Soviet motivations and aims and any prospect for mutual accommodation. A large number of current and former senior officials and some outside experts were brought into the exercise, which was successfully conducted in secrecy from the initial discussion in May to the final reporting in September.[24] The two principal outcomes of Project Solarium were (1) a reaffirmation of the policy of containment, or perhaps "containment plus," although not so identified, of course, rather than the setting of a clear course for liberation, and (2) a decision to rely more heavily on nuclear deterrence and on the possibility of nuclear response even to nonnuclear threats to American interests around the globe, the strategic New Look. These guidelines were set forth in the revised Basic National Security Policy, NSC 162, in September–October 1953.[25]

The underlying assessment of Soviet objectives was unchanged. So, too, was the broad U.S. aim, which was to reduce "both the ability and the intent of the

23. Eisenhower, *Mandate for Change*, p. 254; emphasis added.
24. See *FRUS 1952–1954*, vol. 2, pp. 323–31, 349–54, 360–66, 387–440. The project acquired its code name from the initial discussion of the idea in the White House solarium.
25. See ibid., pp. 489–534, 565–67, 577–87. For a useful discussion of Project Solarium based on additional sources, see Richard H. Immerman, "Confessions of an Eisenhower Revisionist: An Agonizing Reappraisal," *Diplomatic History,* vol. 14 (Summer 1990), pp. 335–42.

Kremlin to exercise this [Soviet] power so as to threaten free world security."
According to the BNSP, the United States should "seek to convince the Kremlin of
the fallacy of the fundamental concepts upon which their policies are based."
At the same time, the "vulnerabilities of the Soviet Bloc should be exploited by
various covert and overt means."[26]

Soviet flexibility and moves toward more cooperative and less threatening
policies were regarded not only with suspicion, but as an obstacle to American
interests rather than steps toward accommodation. The BNSP acknowledged
"significant fluctuations of Soviet policy in the direction of a more disarming
posture" and warned that "the U.S. must be careful how we treat such relaxations
of the Soviet attitude. It is extremely important that we do not appear to show
ourselves as the people who want the cold war to continue, or the people who
appear to lag behind the Soviet leaders in their readiness to effect the solution
of outstanding problems by negotiation. We must have an effective *stance* with
relation to the problem of negotiation."[27]

The Eisenhower administration and above all the president himself did not,
in fact, want the cold war to continue, and some at least did want to negotiate
(albeit from strength). The problem was that the American leaders, believing
that the Soviet leaders were committed to permanent hostility and rivalry,
evaluated Soviet overtures and accommodations not as a new policy course,
but as tactical measures to weaken the West (or, more often in the mid-1950s,
"the Free World"). For example, a National Intelligence Estimate issued in
October 1953, after the Solarium exercise and during the preparation of the
new Basic National Security Policy paper, declared that "the Communist leaders will conduct a vigorous political warfare campaign to undermine the
Western power position. At present the Kremlin seems to be trying to give the
impression that it has adopted a more conciliatory policy than that followed in
Stalin's later years. The Kremlin may hope by such tactics to relax the vigilance
of some Western states, to encourage dissension between the U.S. and its allies,
and to delay the progress of Western rearmament."[28]

Accordingly, the new "ostensibly conciliatory tactics" of the Soviet leaders
were thought to "pose a new challenge to the Free World."[29] Soviet efforts to
reduce tensions were seen more as a problem to be met by keeping up the
West's guard than as an opportunity for improving relations. Moreover, the

26. *FRUS 1952–1954*, vol. 2, p. 410.
27. Ibid., p. 411; emphasis in the original.
28. NIE 99, October 23, 1953, in ibid., pp. 554; see also NSC 162/2, October 30, 1953, ibid.,
pp. 579, 584.
29. Ibid., p. 552.

more that Eisenhower, Dulles, and others in the administration became concerned with vulnerabilities in Western unity, the more inclined they were to think that Soviet policy was aimed precisely at disrupting the unity of the free world. To a certain extent this was correct, but Soviet efforts to weaken their adversary sprang from defensive as well as offensive motives, and this was rarely the sole Soviet diplomatic objective.

The underlying assumption that the Soviet threat was implacable drove American attention and policies toward building up the strength of the United States and the free world and attempting by adversarial means short of war to weaken the Soviet bloc. There remained an ambivalence toward the idea that negotiations, disarmament agreements, and other nonconfrontational means could also reduce tensions and the threat. President Eisenhower himself, and his administration, did try to find areas of congruent interest and did negotiate such measures as the Austrian state treaty. But the attempts to pursue initiatives of this kind, even the proposals for cooperation, were almost always outweighed by or overburdened with an offensive political edge. The example of the Atoms for Peace initiative cited earlier was but the first.

Eisenhower and Dulles expected little from negotiations in their time—and got little—but it remains to be demonstrated that Soviet policy would have permitted much more. To their credit, both President Eisenhower and Dulles did believe that in the long run negotiations could come to play an important role, which marked a distinct step forward from the position taken in NSC 68.[30] Also, they did not see a military solution to the East-West conflict as an alternative to waging the cold war and waiting for a more propitious time for negotiated settlements.

In July 1955, when the multilateral summit finally took place in Geneva, President Eisenhower, seeking to advance negotiations on disarmament and European security, again put forward a dramatic initiative. After bypassing most of the government in Washington and giving only short notice to British Foreign Minister Anthony Eden, Eisenhower outlined what soon became known as the Open Skies proposal for reciprocal aerial surveillance. The speech was a resounding success in public diplomacy; it was flatly rejected by Moscow. At the same time, it was a massive diversion from the move toward disarmament inspection and reductions that the Soviet Union had made in Geneva two months

30. This point has also been made by John Lewis Gaddis, *Strategies of Containment: A Critical Appraisal of Postwar American National Security Policy* (Oxford University Press, 1982), pp. 160–61.

earlier, on May 10, to which the West never responded constructively.[31] The idea, originated by Nelson Rockefeller (who had succeeded C. D. Jackson as the psychological warfare and cold war planner), had been opposed by the State Department and initially by Secretary Dulles.[32]

Some Soviet commentators in later years suggested that the real purpose behind the Open Skies proposal was to lay the groundwork for the covert American unilateral air reconnaissance that began soon after.[33] The available record does not support that contention, but some key members of the administration, above all the president, were aware of the preparations for the covert U.S. program. In fact, the first test flight of the U-2 aircraft occurred only two weeks after the president's speech, and the first operational flight to penetrate Soviet air space came the following July. Meanwhile, an interim (and not very successful) program overflying the USSR with large balloons carrying sophisticated pre-programmed cameras (code-named Genetrix) began in November 1955. Moreover, when the U.S. U-2 program became known and ended in May 1960, the Open Skies proposal was cited defensively as evidence of a prior American attempt to get an agreement.[34] Nonetheless, those covert intelligence collection programs would have proceeded without the speech, and the speech would almost certainly have been made without the programs—its original proponents were not aware of the tightly held plans for the U-2 program.

Open Skies, like Atoms for Peace, was intended to put the Soviet Union on the defensive over its closed society. President Eisenhower expected the proposal to be rejected, and, after discussing it with Khrushchev in Geneva, he concluded that indeed the main problem was the Soviet leader's determination "to keep the USSR a closed society."[35] That was true, but the reason may not have been ideological, as Eisenhower believed. Khrushchev's main concern was probably the security imperative of keeping secret Soviet military weakness

31. For the text of the Soviet proposal of May 10, 1955, see *Documents on Disarmament, 1945–1957*, vol. 1 (Department of State, 1960), pp. 456–67.

32. The fullest account of the origins and development of the Open Skies idea is in W. W. Rostow, *Open Skies: Eisenhower's Proposal of July 21, 1955* (University of Texas Press, 1982).

33. The most authoritative was a confidential internal discussion in the restricted-circulation General Staff journal *Military Thought*, not heretofore available in the West. See Major General S. Kholdin and Lt. Colonel G. Petrov, "'Open Skies' in the Aggressive Plans of American Imperialism," *Voyennaya mysl'*, no. 8 (August 1960), pp. 46–56. For an interesting recent Soviet research study and analysis of the origins and motivations of the U.S. proposal, see Vladislav M. Zubok, "The Sky above the 'Superpowers' (A Prehistory of 'Open Skies')," *SShA: Ekonomika, politika, ideologiya* (USA: economics, politics and ideology), no. 7 (July 1990), pp. 47–55.

34. See part 2.

35. Eisenhower, *Mandate for Change*, p. 522.

and vulnerability. Indeed, the president's proposal called not only for aerial reconnaissance, but also for each party to provide "a complete blueprint of our military establishments, from beginning to end, from one end of our countries to the other."[36] This dimension of the proposal, by the way, was not known or approved in advance by the U.S. Joint Chiefs of Staff (JCS); only the idea of aerial reconnaissance had been discussed with Admiral Arthur Radford, chairman of the JCS.

When Khrushchev's secret speech to the Soviet Communist party congress in February 1956 denouncing Stalin's repressions was acquired by U.S. intelligence, the president and Secretary Dulles decided to publish it in order to put the Soviet leadership on the defensive at home and around the world. Although policymakers devoted a good deal of attention to how best to exploit the propaganda opportunity, virtually none was directed to the significance of the speech as a possible turning point in the evolution of the Soviet system and in Soviet policies.

While not expecting much better relations with the Soviet Union (for example, when the president finally went to the summit in 1955, he expected at best only some "tactical changes" in Soviet policy), the Eisenhower administration also did not expect the worst—war.[37] To be sure, this assessment was attributed not to Soviet self-restraint, but to the effect of countervailing strengths—especially superior American military power.

The administration's assessment of the adversary concluded that the Soviet leaders did not intend to launch a general nuclear war in the near future. In the words of an NIE in October 1953: "We believe that deliberate initiation of general war by the USSR is unlikely in this period" and that the Soviet leaders would "try to avoid courses of action which in their judgment might involve substantial risk of general war."[38] This marked a continuation of the position taken in U.S. intelligence estimates ever since the cold war began, which had been stated in the same terms in the last estimate under the Truman administration.[39]

36. See *FRUS 1955–1957* (1988), vol. 5, p. 452.

37. For his expectations with respect to the 1955 summit, see Eisenhower, *Mandate for Change*, p. 506. With respect to his views on the possibility of war, in addition to the formal estimates cited below, President Eisenhower was strongly convinced that the Soviet leaders would not attack the West.

38. *FRUS 1952–1954*, vol. 2, pp. 551, 554. The intelligence representative of the JCS dissented on this as on some other occasions, holding that intelligence on Soviet intentions and capabilities was "insufficient" to justify an estimate that deliberate initiation of general war was unlikely.

39. "Estimate of the World Situation through 1954," November 21, 1952, ibid., p. 187. This particular paper was an estimate by the Board of National Estimates, not coordinated with all intelligence agencies as an NIE, but this judgment was not new or at variance with earlier NIEs.

Of course, the intelligence estimates also noted the "continuing danger that it [general war] may occur from a series of actions and counteractions initiated by either side, but not intended by either side to have that result." The danger of a preemptive attack was emphasized: "In particular it [war] might arise from actions by one side that were regarded by the other as an imminent threat to its security."[40]

Although the intelligence estimates drew attention to the dangers of an escalating crisis and of reciprocal actions and counteractions by both sides, policymakers were more concerned about a Soviet miscalculation of U.S. and free world strength and resolve. Political leaders, including President Eisenhower and Secretary Dulles, were especially concerned about Soviet evaluations of U.S. intentions, rather than deterrence capabilities, and therefore pressed for firm if not strident declarations of readiness for retaliation at times and places of U.S. choosing. Military leaders tended to be more concerned about building military capabilities to influence Soviet assessments and reduce the Soviet threat. Thus, in an NSC meeting on March 31, 1953, considering early measures to reduce military spending, Secretary Dulles stressed that while strength was necessary, "the greatest danger of such a [global] war would come from Soviet miscalculation of the intentions of the United States." The same danger was seen for local aggression: "There must be no repetition of the fuzzy situation in Korea in the spring of 1950, which constituted an invitation to the Soviets to move against South Korea."[41]

The concern of the American leaders over Soviet miscalculation of American intentions or resolve was not accompanied by any recognition of the danger that *American* miscalculation of Soviet aims could lead to courses of action that might heighten the Soviet perceptions of an American threat to their security.

The Eisenhower administration did move in its first two years to improve its threat assessments in two ways. First, estimates were no longer keyed to a presumed future "year of greatest danger." Second, building on a last-minute initiative by the outgoing administration, efforts were launched to make a *net* assessment of the threat, evaluating Soviet military capabilities not merely on the basis of their increasing forces, but measuring these forces against U.S. and free world forces and the capability of countering and matching them. This helped somewhat to dilute the image of a growing Soviet

40. Ibid., p. 187 (for the November 1952 estimate), and pp. 551–52 (for the October 1953 NIE).

41. Ibid., pp. 265–66.

juggernaut.[42] Such net assessments did not, however, consider intentions or take into account strategic interrelationships except in the course of war gaming.[43]

President Eisenhower and Secretary Dulles were both confident that the Soviet leaders would not launch an attack. They were concerned about the danger of escalation from any lesser military conflict, and about Soviet-controlled communist subversive activities and other aggrandizement. While certainly pursuing a policy based on maintaining nuclear deterrence, Eisenhower in his own assessment probably believed that an existential (if not minimum) nuclear deterrent sufficed.[44]

Throughout the Eisenhower administration, there was a keen awareness of and concern over nuclear parity. Notwithstanding the great U.S. superiority in numbers of nuclear weapons and in strategic strike forces and capabilities, U.S. leaders recognized early on that even continuing superiority would be less meaningful as the Soviet Union acquired a similar, even if smaller, capability. In the words of a National Intelligence Estimate in October 1953:

> The progress being made by the USSR in the development of nuclear weapons is also a factor of prime military and psychological importance in the world situation. As this Soviet capability increases, Western superiority in numbers of nuclear weapons will be of relatively less significance as far as the psychological factor is concerned. As the USSR increases its capabilities for delivering a seriously damaging attack on the US, the US is losing the unique position it has held in the East-West struggle. The full impact of this development is not yet clear.[45]

42. On its last day in office, the outgoing administration issued NSC 140, an NSC directive creating a Special Evaluation Subcommittee to evaluate the Soviet net capability to damage the United States. See ibid., pp. 205–207, 328–49, 367–70. This net estimating approach was carried further in 1954; see the account of a key participant, Ray S. Cline, *Secrets, Spies and Scholars: Blueprint of the Essential CIA* (Washington: Acropolis Books, 1976), pp. 140–43. See also *FRUS 1955–1957*, vol. 19, pp. 56–57, 187–91, 379–81, 672–76.

43. The administration also convened a special panel of experts, called the Technical Capabilities Panel, to evaluate the military threat with more salutary results than such committees usually yield. It was called the Killian Committee after its chairman, James Killian of the Massachusetts Institute of Technology—later to become the first presidential science adviser. The report, "Meeting the Threat of Surprise Attack," helped provide a sound basis for future military programming. The Killian Committee report is printed in *FRUS 1955–1957*, vol. 19, pp. 41–56. See also James R. Killian, Jr., *Sputnik, Scientists and Eisenhower: A Memoir of the First Special Assistant to the President for Science and Technology* (MIT Press, 1977).

44. For a similar conclusion based on Eisenhower's unpublished notes and diaries, see Immerman, "Confessions of an Eisenhower Revisionist," esp. pp. 331, 334.

45. NIE-99, in *FRUS 1952–1954*, vol. 2, p. 552.

The main concern, as noted in another NIE a year later, was that the Soviet Union might suppose it had "greater freedom of action to pursue its objectives without running substantial risk of general war."[46] This was translated in the next BNSP into a lead sentence declaring that "the Soviet-Communist challenge, including the approach of the USSR to nuclear plenty, constitutes a peril greater than any the United States has ever before faced."[47] And in a meeting with congressional leaders in December 1954, President Eisenhower—speaking, as he himself chose to put it, as commander-in-chief—described the "basic change" in the military picture as one of "fear having appeared for the first time in the United States, since it was no longer immune from attack," and he therefore stressed maintaining military strength for deterrence.[48]

The NSC's Basic National Security Policy paper prepared at the end of 1954 acknowledged for the first time the approach of a situation in which general nuclear war "would bring about such extreme destruction as to threaten the survival of both Western civilization and the Soviet system. This situation could create a condition of mutual deterrence, in which each side would be strongly inhibited from deliberately initiating general war or taking actions which it regarded as materially increasing the risk of general war." War would still be possible, "if only because of the element of [possible] miscalculation by either side," but also because of what was seen as a new future danger, "a technological breakthrough by the Soviets leading them to believe they could destroy the United States without effective retaliation."[49] This latter theme would become more important in the second Eisenhower administration.

The more immediate policy issue throughout the first Eisenhower administration was the extent to which the United States should use strategic superiority to press the Soviet Union, or to negotiate. To a limited extent, the administration did both, but on the whole refrained from either.

46. NIE 11-5-54, "Soviet Capabilities and Main Lines of Policy through Mid-1959," June 7, 1954, *FRUS 1952–1954*, vol. 8, pp. 1236–37; and see NSC 5422, June 14, 1954, *FRUS 1952–1954*, vol. 2, p. 653.

47. NSC 5440, "Basic National Security Policy," *FRUS 1952–1954*, vol. 2, p. 808. NSC 5440/1, approved on December 28, 1954 (with this sentence cited unchanged), was reissued as NSC 5501, January 7, 1955, and served as the BNSP for 1955. See *FRUS 1955–1957*, vol. 19, pp. 24–38.

48. *FRUS 1952–1954*, vol. 2, pp. 825–26. There was also concern over the impact on U.S. allies of the growing Soviet (and for that matter combined Soviet and American) nuclear power. A National Intelligence Estimate, NIE 100-54, "Probable Effects of Increasing Nuclear Capabilities upon the Policies of U.S. Allies," was prepared in April 1954. See ibid., pp. 646–47.

49. NSC 5440, December 14, 1954, in ibid., pp. 808–09; carried over into NSC 5501, January 7, 1955, *FRUS 1955–1957*, vol. 19, p. 26.

Despite the rollback rhetoric, the Eisenhower administration was much more constrained in its actions than its predecessor had been. From 1949 until 1953, the United States had air-dropped agents into the USSR, including liaison with resistance forces in Lithuania until 1952 and the Ukraine until 1953.[50] In addition, more extensive covert actions in Eastern Europe included supplying agents, men, and arms to an anticommunist opposition movement in Poland from 1950 until 1952 (when it was discovered to have been controlled by the UB, the Polish security service). An attempt was mounted, with the British, to overthrow the communist government in Albania from 1948 to 1952, but it was unsuccessful (in part because the British intelligence control officer, Kim Philby, was a Soviet agent).[51]

These and other activities were undertaken under NSC guidance of 1949, which had concluded that "the time is ripe for us to place greater emphasis on the offensive to consider whether we cannot do more to cause the elimination or at least the reduction of predominant Soviet influence in the satellite states of Eastern Europe."[52]

In an early meeting of the National Security Council, in March 1953, Secretary Dulles talked about ways of "ending the peril represented by the Soviet Union," which he suggested "could be done by inducing the disintegration of Soviet power." "If we keep our pressures on, psychological and otherwise," he urged, "we may either force a collapse of the Kremlin regime or else transform the Soviet orbit from a union of satellites dedicated to aggression, into a coalition for defense only," but "we must not relax this pressure until the Soviets give promise of ending the struggle." Furthermore, "the President emphatically endorsed Secretary Dulles' warning against any relaxation of pressure on the USSR."[53]

In its first month in office, the Eisenhower administration supported a move in Congress to pass a resolution condemning Soviet domination of the "captive nations" of Eastern Europe, but it failed because of a partisan division: Republicans objected to its failure to repudiate the Yalta agreements, while Democrats opposed its implied criticism of the Roosevelt and Truman administrations.[54] A similar rhetorical resolution

50. See Harry Rositzke, *The CIA's Secret Operations* (New York: Reader's Digest, 1977), pp. 168–69. Rositzke was a senior CIA covert operations officer during this period.

51. On both operations, see ibid., pp. 169–72.

52. NSC 58/2, "United States Policy toward the Soviet Satellite States in Eastern Europe," December 8, 1949, in *FRUS 1949* (1976), vol. 5, p. 43.

53. *FRUS 1952–1954*, vol. 2, pp. 267–68.

54. Gaddis, *Strategies of Containment*, p. 155.

was adopted in 1959 and—though now an anachronism—remains operative to this day.

In practice, however, the Eisenhower administration showed great caution, notwithstanding its earlier strident electoral rhetoric. The NSC Basic National Security Policy paper issued after the Solarium review gave little leeway to "liberation," in large part because of its assessment that "the detachment of any major European satellite from the Soviet bloc does not now appear feasible except by Soviet acquiescence or war."[55] The Soviet Union had demonstrated in East Berlin in June 1953 that it could suppress any popular uprising, and the Eisenhower administration ruled out war. Policy guidance, however, was ambiguous. An NSC policy paper in 1954 continued to state that "although the time for a significant rollback of Soviet power may appear to be in the future, the U.S. should be prepared, by feasible current actions or future planning, to take advantage of an earlier opportunity to contest Communist-controlled areas and power."[56]

Nonetheless, when Hungary sought to withdraw from the Warsaw Pact and Soviet domination in November 1956, the restrained general assessment of NSC 162/2, Soviet unpreparedness to acquiesce, and American unreadiness to intervene and risk war were all confirmed.

In other parts of the world, the Eisenhower administration was much more prepared to resort to covert operations. This approach rested, in important part, on a judgment that this was the ground on which the Soviet Union was waging the cold war. In an NSC meeting in late 1954, while arguing against the idea that the Soviet leaders were disposed to military action, Secretary Dulles stated: "The verdict of history was that the Soviet leaders had been rather cautious in exercising their power. They were not reckless, as Hitler was; but primarily they rely not on military force but on methods of subversion."[57] One lesson drawn was, in Dulles's words: "Hence, if areas exposed to the Communist threat can build up governments capable of maintaining internal security and governments which can't be overthrown except by overt, brutal acts of aggression, it will be possible to withstand the present Soviet threat."[58] This

55. NSC 162/2, October 30, 1953, in *FRUS 1952–1954*, vol. 2, p. 580. This judgment was repeated in subsequent policy papers; for example, the OCB "Analysis of the Situation with Respect to Possible Detachment of a Major European Soviet Satellite," January 5, 1955, *FRUS 1955–1957* (1990), vol. 25, p. 9.

56. NSC 5422/2, August 7, 1954, and NSC policy paper, October 1954, *FRUS 1952–1954*, vol. 2, pp. 720, 746.

57. Ibid., p. 847.

58. Ibid., pp. 841–42.

line of reasoning, shared by President Eisenhower, led not only to full support for strengthening NATO, but also to the creation in the 1950s of other regional alliances—notably the Central Treaty Organization in the Middle East (CENTO) (after an earlier abortive attempt in the short-lived Baghdad Pact) and the Southeast Asia Treaty Organization (SEATO).

This line of reasoning also led to the expansion of American covert operations, to fighting fire with fire. Comprehensive consolidated NSC guidelines (NSC 5412) were issued in March 1954, specifying a wide range of activities in addition to political action and economic warfare, such as "subversion against hostile states or groups including assistance to underground resistance movements, guerrilla and refugee liberation groups; support of indigenous and anti-communist elements in threatened countries of the free world; deception plans and operations; and all activities compatible with this directive necessary to accomplish the foregoing."[59]

In 1953, not long before this directive was issued, the United States (with Britain) had arranged the overthrow of Mohammed Mossadeq and the return of the shah of Iran; and three months later, the CIA engineered the overthrow of the elected government of Guatemala's leftist president Jacobo Guzman Arbenz. It also attempted to overthrow Sukarno in Indonesia in 1958, without success, and in 1960–61 was preparing an émigré Cuban military force to challenge Castro in Cuba. It sent irregular guerrilla forces into southern China, Tibet, and North Vietnam in the 1950s. It became involved in assassination plots against Fidel Castro, Patrice Lumumba, and Rafael Trujillo.

The administration tended to view all third world issues through the prism of the cold war with Moscow.[60] Thus, when the Soviet Union established more normal and active foreign relations with the countries of Asia and Africa, this was seen as presaging subversion. Among the danger signals detected in Washington were the visit of Khrushchev and Nikolai Bulganin to India, Burma, and Afghanistan in 1955, and the supply of arms by Czechoslovakia to Nasser's Egypt in 1955 and by the Soviet Union to Afghanistan soon after (only after the United States, owing to its new alliance with Afghanistan's rival Pakistan, had rebuffed Afghan overtures). This concern intensified after the nonaligned movement arose in the third world in opposition to America's alliance pacts. The Soviet diplomatic campaign was aided by U.S. opposition

59. NSC 5412, "Covert Operations," March 15, 1954, pp. 2–3; Top Secret, now declassified, but not published in *FRUS*.

60. For a good brief review, see Robert J. McMahon, "Eisenhower and Third World Nationalism: A Critique of the Revisionists," *Political Science Quarterly*, vol. 101 (Fall 1986), pp. 453–73.

to neutrality while the Soviet Union championed it, winning wide noncommunist support in the emerging postcolonial nations. When Middle Eastern ferment boiled over in Iraq in 1958, concern in the West led to the dramatic landing of American marines and soldiers in Lebanon (and British troops in Jordan). Later, the success of Castro in Cuba and his steady drift toward alignment with the Soviet Union in 1959–61 was a particularly sore point with the Eisenhower administration (and its successors).

Nor was the European theater of the cold war forgotten. By 1955–56, the CIA was again preparing émigré East Europeans for possible action. After the Polish demonstrations in Poznan in the summer of 1956, the CIA reportedly dispatched some Hungarians to their homeland and prepared also to send in some Czechoslovaks and Romanians.[61] The Hungarian revolution of October–November 1956 stopped that program. When faced with a genuine Eastern European revolt and Soviet armed suppression, the administration wisely concluded that it could not intervene and should not stimulate such situations.

Although those in charge of covert action had prepared for and expected an opportunity to stir things up in Eastern Europe, the intelligence analysts and estimators had failed to foresee the Polish and Hungarian eruptions of 1956. A National Intelligence Estimate the preceding year had said flatly, "Popular resistance of an organized and active kind is unlikely to appear in any of the Satellites during the period of this estimate [1955–60]."[62] Only months before Poznan and Budapest, the latest NIE forecasting developments in Eastern Europe expressed the view that "no development short of a drastic impairment of Communist controls or the approach of friendly forces in time of war would be sufficient to stimulate important outbreaks of open resistance."[63]

A year after the events of 1956, the annual Soviet NIE correctly predicted continued Soviet control of the bloc over at least the five years covered by the estimate, despite "further instability in the states of Eastern Europe and in their relations with the USSR," and noted that Moscow had not recognized the "ferment evoked by the denunciation of Stalinism at the XXth Party Congress" until it was too late.[64]

61. See William R. Corson, *The Armies of Ignorance: The Rise of the American Intelligence Empire* (Dial, 1977), pp. 366–72.

62. NIE 11-3-55, *Soviet Capabilities and Probable Soviet Courses of Action through 1960*, May 17, 1955, p. 10; Top Secret, declassified; not printed in *FRUS 1955–1957*.

63. NIE 12-56, "Probable Developments in the European Satellites through 1960," January 10, 1956, in *FRUS 1955–1957*, vol. 25, p. 117; and see NSC 5608/1, "Statement of Policy on U.S. Policy toward the Soviet Satellites in Eastern Europe," July 18, 1956, ibid., pp. 217–21.

64. NIE 11-4-57, paras. 167, 169, p. 40. This part of the NIE was not printed in *FRUS 1955–1957*.

The other important member of the communist camp was China. Policy guidance acknowledged the possibility and desirability of fissures developing between Moscow and Beijing.[65] But there was a considerable gap between the assessments of policymakers and the public, both of whom stressed "the communist world" and "the Soviet bloc" (including China) as *the* adversary, and the assessment of intelligence analysts (and those American diplomats expert on China who had survived the McCarthyite purge), who saw an alliance of two communist powers with a mix of common and differing interests. It is now known that divergences in Soviet-Chinese relations always existed and grew in the Eisenhower years from friction in the mid-1950s to an open rift in 1960. The National Intelligence Estimates in the 1950s did not foresee a Sino-Soviet split, although they did recognize separate decisions and some differences.

The second major area of assessment, apart from the strengths and weaknesses of the Soviet Union and Soviet bloc, was Soviet military power. The increasing Soviet nuclear capability prompted heightened efforts in intelligence collection. There was widespread use of legal travelers in the USSR, peripheral reconnaissance flights and incursions into territorial waters, a tunnel burrowed into East Berlin to tap into the Soviet military telephone cable lines (uncovered in April 1956), and other such efforts.[66] Most notable and successful, although ultimately most politically damaging, was the deep penetration of Soviet airspace with high-altitude U-2 photographic reconnaissance air missions, from July 1956 to May 1960. Although the Soviet Union was unable to interdict these flights, it did track them and was thus aware of the program. The U.S. Strategic Air Command also flew some penetrating reconnaissance overflights, and in at least one case in the 1950s made a demonstration flight over the Vladivostok defense region, apparently without political authorization.[67]

65. The BNSP of October 1953, NSC 162/2, had acknowledged that "in the long run, basic differences may strain or break the [Sino-Soviet] alliance," but it emphasized that the alliance was "based on common ideology," as well as "the current community of interests," and appears to be "firmly established." *FRUS 1952–1954*, vol. 2, p. 580.

Incidentally, under the traditional transcription system then in general use, Beijing was "Peking." In official U.S. government documents, the usual name used for the city in the 1950s was, however, "Peiping." Peking means "northern capital," and rather than consent even to that degree of recognition, the older name Peiping, meaning "northern city," was preferred. Mainland China was always referred to as "Communist China."

66. For a fairly comprehensive review, see Jeffrey Richelson, *American Espionage and the Soviet Target* (Quill/William Morrow, 1987).

67. See the disclosure by General Curtis LeMay, in Richard H. Kohn and Joseph P. Hanrahan, eds., "U.S. Strategic Air Power, 1948–1962: Excerpts from an Interview with Generals Curtis E. LeMay, Leon W. Johnson, David A. Burchinal, and Jack A. Catton," *International Security*, vol. 12 (Spring 1988), p. 86.

The Eisenhower administration was prepared to wage the political cold war and to take the necessary military preparation and intelligence measures, but it did not embark on a program of military pressure. Admiral Radford and his colleagues at the Joint Chiefs of Staff more than once raised the matter, but the administration rejected such a course. In November 1954, for example, Secretary of Defense Charles Wilson forwarded to the NSC (with his own endorsement) JCS comments criticizing the application of basic national security policy and calling for interpretation of its terms to allow a more "dynamic," "positive," and less "reactive" policy—in effect, a policy of coercion rather than passive deterrence.

This recommendation for a changed policy was based on a divergent and more ominous assessment of both Soviet strengths and free world weaknesses. Going beyond the National Intelligence Estimates and NSC BNSPs, the JCS characterized Soviet policy as prepared, if necessary, to use military force to achieve its objectives: "There is no acceptable evidence of abandonment or major modification of the Communist objective of achieving ultimate world domination, using armed force, if necessary." With Soviet military capabilities increasing, "this combination of objective and capabilities together comprise a threat to the non-Communist world in general, and to our national security in particular." In the view of the JCS, the increasing Soviet nuclear capability was causing a growing fear of nuclear war in other countries and was creating "a definite trend toward neutralism" in the noncommunist world.[68]

The JCS cited the current BNSP, NSC 162/2, stating the U.S. aim was to build "the free world coalition . . . to meet the Soviet-Communist threat with resolution" before nuclear parity and mutual deterrence ("mutual nuclear plenty") were reached. But, the JCS contended, in the year since the guidance, "the Soviet-Communist threat has not been reduced, while the time available for the establishment of more secure conditions has appreciably diminished."[69] What was their answer?

The United States rejects the concept of preventive war or acts intended to provoke war. Thus, a definite limit is established beyond which our policy and courses of action to implement that policy should not go. However, there remains a wide latitude between a category of somewhat passive measures which are reactive or counteractive to Soviet acts or threats of aggression and a category of more positive measures to be undertaken "even at the risk of but without deliberately provoking war." . . . It is clear that steps taken under NSC 162/2 have not resulted in a reduction of the Soviet-Communist

68. *FRUS 1952–1954*, vol. 2, p. 785.
69. Ibid., p. 786.

threat. On the contrary, NSC 162/2 as basic security policy has been attended by continued emphasis on reactive-type security measures and continued growth of the threat to the free world. Accordingly, it is believed necessary to remove from NSC 162/2 its present preponderant commitment to a policy of reaction, with the purpose of providing a basic U.S. security policy of unmistakably positive quality.[70]

The JCS was rebuffed in its attempt to turn U.S. national security policy from a reactive stance to an initiative with "more positive measures to be undertaken 'even at the risk of but without deliberately provoking war.'"

Although Admiral Radford did not specify what he had in mind, it was quite likely that he and the JCS were thinking of such things as an extraordinary Air Force proposal for controlling Soviet behavior by U.S. unilateral domination and air patrol of Soviet air space. The idea was to compel the Soviet Union, by ultimatums (backed by U.S. control of the skies), to accept peace treaties with Germany, Austria, and Japan on U.S. terms, which included Soviet military withdrawal from Germany and its unification, the establishment of noncommunist governments in Eastern Europe, abrogation of the Sino-Soviet treaty, and acceptance of the Baruch plan for nuclear disarmament. If necessary, graduated air strikes would be undertaken. The proposal was based on a British concept for policing distant colonial or subject territories in the Middle East in the 1920s and early 1930s called "air control" and thus became known as Project Control. While the idea was breathtaking in its ambitious scope (and irresponsible naïveté), what was no less extraordinary was that it was given a hearing by various senior U.S. officials, of whom the most receptive were Admiral Radford and the Joint Chiefs of Staff at a briefing given on August 26, 1954. The Air Force authors of the project had described it as a "positive" line of action, and with a little stretching it could be said to fit Admiral Radford's call for positive measures "even at the risk of but without deliberately provoking war." Needless to say, Project Control was never adopted by the government.[71] It was, as State Department policy planner Robert Bowie remarked, "simply

70. Ibid.

71. For a comprehensive look at this bizarre episode, based on interviews and the declassified twenty-two volumes of files on the project, see Tami Davis Biddle, "Handling the Soviet Threat: 'Project Control' and the Debate on American Strategy in the Early Cold War Years," *Journal of Strategic Studies,* vol. 12 (September 1989), pp. 273–302. I was present at one of the Project Control briefings, on July 7, 1954. Admiral Radford, when he heard the Project Control briefing in 1954, stated his belief that "if the U.S. did not adopt and successfully follow through on a course of action similar to Project Control, that in the period mid 1957–1960 there would

another version of preventive war."[72] And the Eisenhower administration, after some earlier equivocation, had explicitly rejected the idea of preventive war by late 1954.[73]

In the NSC discussion of the JCS position, Secretary John Foster Dulles disarmingly acknowledged that "he could not help but have some sympathy for the general view of the Joint Chiefs of Staff in favor of greater dynamism in the American attitude toward the Soviet Union and Communist China. After all, during the course of the 1952 campaign he had himself called for a more dynamic U.S. policy vis-à-vis Communism. However, experience indicated that it was not easy to go very much beyond the point that this Administration had reached in translating a dynamic policy into courses of action, and in any case we had been more dynamic than our predecessors."[74] He said that stronger measures, for example, "to overthrow the Communist regimes in China and in the European satellites . . . would involve the United States in general war." But even if successful without war, they would not deal with what he termed "the heart of the problem," the Soviet nuclear capability. Nor did he believe in a policy of ultimatums. Finally, in a prescient prediction, he argued that "one could properly anticipate that there will be in the future some disintegration of the present monolithic power structure of the Soviet orbit," for example, Chinese

---

be either an all-out atomic war or the U.S. would be forced into an agreement which would mean victory for the USSR." See ibid., pp. 292–301.

72. Ibid., p. 291.

73. See NSC 5440, *FRUS 1952–1954*, vol. 2, p. 815. For a review of American official thinking about preventive war, see Russell D. Buhite and Wm. Christopher Hamel, "War for Peace: The Question of an American Preventive War against the Soviet Union, 1945–1955," *Diplomatic History*, vol. 14 (Summer 1990), pp. 367–84.

President Eisenhower himself, in a pessimistic moment in September 1953, wrote in a note to Secretary Dulles that the economic and political burden of deterrence might become so onerous that "we would be forced to consider whether or not our duty to future generations did not require us to initiate war at the most propitious moment that we could designate." See ibid., p. 381. But in policy consideration he always rejected the idea.

At no time did the Eisenhower administration or any other American administration prepare a "war plan" for a deliberate initiation of war. Contingency war plans were prepared for various dates selected only as planning assumptions, not predicted dates for war, and still less as U.S. "target dates" for launching a war. *Dropshot*, a 1949 war plan with a planning assumption of war in 1957, declassified in 1977, is the most notorious. Many Soviet accounts, from ignorance or malice, have misrepresented these as American "plans for war," rather than contingency plans for programming purposes. See the discussion in Raymond L. Garthoff, "Soviet Perceptions of Western Strategic Thought and Doctrine," in Gregory Flynn, ed., *Soviet Military Doctrine and Western Policy* (London and New York: Routledge, 1989), pp. 220–26, 295–97.

74. *FRUS 1952–1954*, vol. 2, p. 833. These remarks, in an NSC meeting on December 21, 1954, are cited from the NSC record, but are not necessarily verbatim.

independence and nationalism among the European satellites that would tend to inhibit the Soviet Union from acting and thus diminish its threat.[75] The president, although he did not directly address this point in the debate, clearly did not support the JCS.

There was a parallel debate over the value of negotiation. The JCS had also objected to proposed language that guardedly suggested there was some value in negotiating with the Soviet Union. There was general agreement on two sentences:

> The U.S. should be ready to negotiate with the USSR whenever it clearly appears that U.S. security interests will be served thereby. The U.S. should continue to take the initiative in advancing proposals for constructive settlements and international cooperation (i.e., atoms for peace) in order to put the Soviets on the defensive and win public support on both sides of the Iron Curtain.

The State Department wanted also to state that "the U.S. should actively use negotiation in pursuing its strategy," "without relaxing its defense posture," and chiefly in order "to expose the Communists' 'conciliatory' line and place on them the onus for the persistence of tension and unsettled problems." Beyond that, however, the State Department wanted to say that

> The U.S. should: (1) seek to settle specific problems, (such as Germany) compatible with U.S. security, (2) seek to achieve a modus vivendi which would reduce world tensions and contribute to free world security; (3) put forward and seek agreement on proposals which, if accepted, would reduce the magnitude of the Soviet-Communist threat (such as an acceptable plan for limitation of armaments with adequate safeguards).

The JCS objected to those statements and wanted to add: "For the most part, however, the U.S. must realize it will be not only fruitless, but perhaps even hazardous, to continue its efforts to arrive at solutions to world problems through the normal processes of negotiation with the USSR." This addition would, of course, have gutted the first agreed sentence expressing readiness to negotiate. The issue was resolved in time-honored bureaucratic fashion—on Secretary Dulles's suggestion, the president decided to drop everything except the first agreed sentence, neither enlarging on nor undercutting it.[76]

75. Ibid., pp. 834, 836.
76. Ibid., pp. 819, 843–44. For a briefer replay of this debate over a year later, see *FRUS 1955–1957*, vol. 19, pp. 222–23, 231.

This and other discussions about negotiation showed that President Eisenhower and Secretary Dulles were keenly interested in negotiation but had low expectations owing to their assessment of Soviet unreadiness for meaningful negotiations to settle issues, a view both held in 1953 and felt was confirmed by the four-power negotiations of 1954 and 1955, the disarmament negotiations, and later negotiations on Berlin in 1958–60. Secretary Dulles, for example, despite his desire to keep open the possibility of negotiation, acknowledged in these NSC discussions that in the 1954–55 Geneva negotiations "we did not actually desire to enter into either negotiation, but felt compelled to do so in order to get our allies to consent to the rearmament of Germany. World opinion demanded that the United States participate in these negotiations with the Communists."[77]

As reflected in the State-JCS divergence over negotiations, the subject of arms control and disarmament was particularly sensitive. There were widespread reservations in the Eisenhower administration about pursuing disarmament. Although some—particularly the main opponent of such negotiations, the Joint Chiefs of Staff—no doubt also had other reasons for their stand, there was a widely shared belief that (as long as the United States refrained from coercion) the Soviet Union would only accept disarmament measures that were clearly to its advantage, and that any such measures would ipso facto be to the disadvantage of the free world. Moreover, the very pursuit of such agreements would give the Soviet leaders the opportunity to employ their sinister and effective propaganda skills. The principal exceptions were the occasional American initiatives calculated by psychological warfare experts to work to U.S. advantage and to be fail-safe, such as Open Skies.

When the Soviet leaders agreed to an Austrian treaty and military withdrawal from Austria, unilateral withdrawal from their base in Finland, and in May 1955 to arms reductions with inspections in Europe, an alarm arose and a retreat from such negotiations was sounded in Washington. When the negotiations resumed in Geneva in the fall of 1955 (having been sidelined during the foreign ministers' meeting and summit in the summer), the U.S. delegation was instructed to "place a reservation" on our own earlier position, in effect repudiating it, and instead to trumpet the Open Skies proposal.[78]

The Soviet major step forward on disarmament on May 10, 1955, did have one important, if not publicly apparent, consequence. It led the Eisenhower

77. *FRUS 1952–1954*, vol. 2, p. 844.
78. For a good review, see Matthew Evangelista, "Cooperation Theory and Disarmament Negotiations in the 1950s," *World Politics*, vol. 42 (June 1990), pp. 502–28.

administration to consider seriously its own attitude toward disarmament, as well as Soviet motivations. In this process, assessment of the Soviet adversary played a most important role. Recently declassified records of NSC meetings and other secret memoranda illuminate the thinking at that time.[79]

The most negative stance was taken by the Joint Chiefs of Staff, supported by Secretary of Defense Charles Wilson. In a memorandum from Wilson to the president on June 28, the chiefs and he argued that *any* attempt at arms control and disarmament "in advance of the settlement of the major political issues causing international tensions is unrealistic and contrary to the best interests of our national security." Deterrence, even mutual deterrence, relying on unilateral and untrammeled American military programs was seen as far preferable to entangling commitments that would make arms control "not a 'fail-safe' course."[80] In an NSC discussion a few days later, Secretary Wilson and Admiral Radford attempted to clarify that perhaps not all issues need be resolved first, but the examples of what should first be resolved were unsettling: "the Iron Curtain should be cracked and reversed," the Russians should disavow the Third International, and China must be included in any arms limitations.[81]

Secretary Dulles, whose own memorandum prepared in advance for use at the meeting had been very reserved, nonetheless took strong issue with the Defense Department position, at which point President Eisenhower interjected to emphasize that he also did not share that view.[82]

In Dulles's opinion, the United States had to support *some* plan for arms limitations so as not to lose the support of its allies and give the Soviet Union a political victory. At the same time, in the words of his memorandum, "we should not seek quickly or radically to alter the present situation," nor take any unnecessary "risks" in pursuit of arms limitations; "present steps to stabilize or curtail armaments should be tentative and exploratory only until good faith and good will are demonstrated by the Soviet Union."[83] His basic view was that the United States could afford to "support indefinitely" an arms race, while "the Soviet Bloc economy cannot indefinitely sustain the effort to match our military output," and "greater military potential . . . gives the United States its maximum bargaining power and this is a power which should not be cheaply

79. See *FRUS 1955–1957* (1990), vol. 20, pp. 76–155. Some specific key statements are cited below.
80. Ibid., pp. 136, 139.
81. Ibid., pp. 146–49.
82. Ibid., p. 146.
83. Ibid., p. 141.

relinquished." He regarded improved Soviet behavior in the post-Stalin period as only making a virtue of necessity given the country's relative weakness, and that "if we wished [Soviet] virtue to continue, we should also continue the pressure of necessity."[84] Dulles did not doubt that "the Soviets genuinely wanted some reductions in the armament burden" and, accordingly, "may be prepared to make concessions."[85] But the United States should "proceed cautiously so long as the present situation gives us important bargaining power and so long as Soviet leadership continues basically hostile, autocratic and controlled by those who are not inhibited by any moral scruples."[86]

If Dulles's memorandum had been circulated beyond his own immediate staff in the State Department, it would no doubt have been seized upon by the advocates of minimal actions in the Pentagon, since it presented a much more sophisticated rationale for holding back from agreeing to disarmament steps, while consistent with Dulles's insistence that the United States adopt a "safe" public *posture* of favoring disarmament. Dulles's own plan was to concentrate on disarmament verification and to ensure that "there should not be any effort to agree upon any overall [disarmament] plan until first a measure of inspection has been tried out and found to be workable." "Concurrently . . . intensive efforts would be made to resolve some of the major political issues such as the armament of Communist China; the Soviet control of the satellites; the promotion of international Communism and the unification of Germany."[87] Although he did not specify a time frame, Dulles was clearly thinking it would take years before any substantial agreement could be reached in the disarmament field.

At the key NSC meeting of June 30, Dulles proposed his new strategy for handling the disarmament issue: to "reverse the process and first study the problem of supervision and policing [verification]," and only later "formulate the plan" for disarmament.[88] The president said he "could not wholly agree" with Dulles, because the disarmament plan and the required verification would be interrelated.[89] Nonetheless, the United States did thereafter, for many years, place strong emphasis on dealing first with the problems of verification, until the Strategic Arms Limitations Talks (SALT) at the end of the 1960s. And the

84. Ibid., pp. 140–41.
85. Ibid., p. 150 (in the NSC meeting June 30, 1955).
86. Ibid., p. 141.
87. Ibid., p. 142.
88. Ibid., p. 151.
89. Ibid., p. 151.

extreme Soviet antipathy to intrusive verification fed this approach until the radical Soviet change on inspection in the latter 1980s.

President Eisenhower was also suspicious of Soviet aims and therefore not sanguine about any early arms agreement. He was, however, far more inclined than Dulles to try to reach agreements as soon as the Soviet Union would come around. Although never (in materials available) presented with Dulles's arguments for keeping U.S. strategic superiority untrammeled, and for pressure and bargaining leverage as well as deterrence, he would not have accepted these arguments, I believe, if there had been a real opportunity for agreement. Nonetheless, Eisenhower, too, because of his perception of the adversary, was led to see the overall U.S.-Soviet relationship and the general stance on negotiations as one requiring the cold war. The record of the June 30, 1955, NSC meeting offers perhaps the clearest statement of his view:

> The President said that at least this much should be clearly understood by everyone present: The Russians were not deserting their Marxian ideology nor their ultimate objectives of world revolution and Communist domination. However, they had found that an arms race was much too expensive a means of achieving these objectives, and they wished to achieve these objectives without recourse to war. If the United States rejects this attitude and seems to prefer a military solution, it would lose the support of the world. Thus our real problem is how we can achieve a stalemate vis-à-vis the Russians in the area of the non-military struggle as we have already achieved such a stalemate in the military field.[90]

The principal diplomatic negotiations with the Soviet Union during the first Eisenhower administration concerned the Austrian treaty, Germany, and European security, as well as disarmament. In addition, there were important diplomatic exchanges over the Korean armistice in 1953, the Vietnam conflict in 1954–55, the Taiwan Straits crisis in 1955, the Suez and Hungarian crises in 1956, and the Middle East crisis of 1956. Meetings and exchanges between foreign ministers and other diplomatic representatives were supplemented by the Geneva four-power summit of July 1955, the first since the end of the war. In addition, an extensive (seventy-two messages) presidential-level correspondence with the Soviet leaders was launched during the first term, in all extending from September 1955 to May 1960 (with Bulganin until March

90. Ibid., p. 152.

1958, thereafter with Prime Minister Khrushchev). This direct Eisenhower–Bulganin/Khrushchev correspondence, however, was public and an orchestrated part of the general pattern of diplomatic interplay, rather than constituting a channel for more meaningful confidential exchanges of the kind that developed in the Kennedy and Nixon administrations. The most discussed issues were disarmament and summitry; some critical issues were not seriously addressed.[91]

Thus the Eisenhower administration in its first term adapted its assessments of the Soviet leadership, objectives, and policies to the post-Stalin era by recognizing a substantial change in Soviet tactics and behavior, but without revising its view of implacable Soviet hostility and ambition based on the pursuit of an ideology proclaiming a worldwide victory for communism. Although the long-term threat remained, by the time of President Eisenhower's reelection in a campaign evidencing a national consensus on the subject, the cold war seemed well under control.

91. For a good review of these exchanges, see Elmer Plischke, "Eisenhower's 'Correspondence Diplomacy' with the Kremlin—Case Study in Summit Diplomatics," *Journal of Politics*, vol. 30 (February 1968), pp. 137–59.

Part 2
The Post-Sputnik Years (1957–61)

There was a pronounced shift both in the U.S. assessment of Soviet intentions and capabilities and in diplomatic initiative and direction roughly from the first to the second Eisenhower administrations. During the years 1953–56, the new Soviet leadership was seeking to establish its legitimacy both at home and in the world. The post-Stalin period of internal political change and maneuver ended with Nikita Khrushchev's denunciation of Stalin's crimes in February 1956 and his victory over the antiparty group combining the factions of Georgy Malenkov and Vyacheslav Molotov in July 1957. During those years, the new collective leadership (under Malenkov as well as Khrushchev, and with their respective colleagues) reoriented Soviet foreign policy to seek détente with the West through the Austrian treaty, disarmament initiatives, and direct diplomatic engagement, and also a new engagement in the third world with arms, aid, and personal diplomacy. Hegemony in Eastern Europe was meanwhile strengthened by making peace with Tito, establishing the Warsaw Pact, and, when it became necessary, suppressing an independent line in Hungary. There were, to be sure, sharp conflicts and even crises, but all in situations beyond Soviet control (the Taiwan Straits crises, Indochina, the Middle East, and in a sense also Hungary).

American assessment of the Soviet Union in 1953–56 was largely directed toward evaluating the significance of the new post-Stalin era. In practice, given the ingrained views of the nature of communism, the real focus was on the tactics of diplomacy of the new leadership. This fitted with an inclination in any case to give principal attention to "building situations of strength" in the free world, the North Atlantic Treaty Organization (NATO), and other alliances, including in particular the full integration of West Germany into the NATO alliance. President Eisenhower sought to build American military power on a foundation of economic strength and hence to give priority to nuclear deterrence. During these years, deterrence seemed unchallenged.

31

The years 1957–60 were marked by several changes, some owing to Soviet decisions to take a more militant stance. Most important was the campaign launched in November 1958 to evict the Western powers from Berlin. It is no exaggeration to say that this political drive dominated Soviet-U.S. and East-West relations from late 1958 until late 1962, nearly two years after the end of the Eisenhower administration. Other developments in the world, often not under Soviet (or U.S.) control, also raised new conflicts in East-West relations, notably the seizure of power in Cuba by Castro in 1959 and his early alignment with the Soviet Union (in 1960–61). Some other situations in the third world, as new nations were emerging from colonialism, also became points of conflict involving the Soviet Union and the West, notably in the Congo and Laos in 1960–61.

There was an ebb and flow in relations between the Soviet Union and the United States during this period. It brought the first in a new series of high-level visits by senior officials of the two countries, including Khrushchev himself in September 1959. The visit by Khrushchev, climaxed by talks with the president at his Camp David retreat, led to a brief détente that was termed "the Spirit of Camp David." But after this and other occasions when relations seemed to be improving, the Soviet leader would again reactivate the campaign over Berlin.

The second major development that created a new framework for U.S.-Soviet relations in the second Eisenhower administration was the Soviet success in first testing an intercontinental ballistic missile (ICBM) and then launching the first Sputnik or artificial satellite in August and October of 1957, respectively. This was a substantial technological achievement, with important military implications, but still more significant by far was its psychological and political impact. It bolstered Soviet confidence that the nation was indeed riding the wave of history, and in particular strengthened Khrushchev's belief that the changing correlation of forces in the world could be jump-started to dramatically demonstrate this Soviet advance. His choice of the key point on which to register this still-emerging Soviet equality was to clean up what, from his point of view, was the anomalous continuing Western presence in Berlin and the West's refusal to recognize the German Democratic Republic (East Germany), preventing consolidation of communist rule in Eastern Europe.

Whereas the Sputnik evoked Russian pride and Soviet self-confidence, it provoked widespread American shock and loss of confidence.[92] Although it

92. The administration had made a deliberate decision in May 1955 to proceed at a normal pace with a U.S. civilian scientific satellite program, called Vanguard, rather than to rush

had some useful consequences—for example, it led Americans to reexamine their educational system and deflated some hubris over a global American century—it also primed exaggerated fears of Soviet military prowess and challenge. American concerns were increased by a policy of deception and bluff Khrushchev adopted to push along Western respect for emerging and potential Soviet missile capabilities by exaggerated claims of their attainment.

Closely following the Soviet Sputnik and ICBM test, an influential special study group earlier commissioned by the president submitted a dire report, the gist of which was promptly leaked to the press. The Gaither Report in November 1957 restored the idea of a year of critical danger and gross exaggeration of the rising Soviet threat. It marked the opening salvo of alarm over a looming "missile gap." While constructing a plausible "capabilities threat," the report cited as a basis for doing so a judgment on Soviet intentions. The consensus on Soviet objectives was evident in the way the report's judgment on intentions was stated: "We have found no evidence in Russian foreign and military policy since 1945 to refute the conclusion that USSR intentions are expansionist, and

---

through the launching of an earth satellite using military rockets (*Thor* or *Jupiter*) in order to be sure of launching the first such satellite. This decision had been made despite recognition that "considerable prestige and psychological benefits will accrue to the nation which first is successful in launching a satellite" and even that the "unmistakable relationship to intercontinental ballistic missile technology might have important repercussions on the political determination of free world countries to resist Communist threats, especially if the USSR were to be the first to establish a satellite." See *FRUS 1955–1957* (1988), vol. 11, p. 725. The Soviets had indicated their own plans for active participation in the International Geophysical Year (beginning July 1957) and were believed to be working on a satellite program. Nonetheless, while some analysts in the scientific and intelligence communities believed the Soviet Union might be able to launch a satellite vehicle before the United States, at the policymaking level there seems to have been an unwarranted assumption that we would be first, stemming from the general assessment of Soviet capabilities. As late as May 1957, when presidential assistant Robert C. Cutler asked Allen Dulles about the Soviet program at an NSC meeting, the latter did not really respond. (See ibid., p. 750.)

From the record, it is clear that mounting costs of the Vanguard program even led the administration to consider canceling it, rather than expanding U.S. efforts. (Ibid., pp. 734–54.) Coupled with an underestimation of Soviet capability, the result was to gloss over the psychological impact of the first launching of an artificial earth satellite, which is rather surprising given the high attention earlier placed on psychological warfare with the Soviet Union.

(In March 1956 in a political war game at RAND, as part of the "Red Team," I had played a Soviet ICBM test and an artificial satellite launching on July 4, 1957—both disallowed by the game umpire, despite my protestation that they were realistic predictions.)

By mid-1957, although an early ICBM test was not yet expected, awareness of intensive Soviet missile development meant that the test was not a great surprise to the analytical intelligence community. But it was a surprise to the American and world publics and probably even to policymakers.

that their great efforts to build military power go beyond any concepts of Soviet defense."[93] The evidence it did find was said to point to peril in the near future: "The evidence clearly indicates an increasing threat which may become critical in 1959 or early 1960."[94] In addition to urging a range of crash military buildup programs, the Gaither Report discreetly called for pressure: "The United States is now capable of making a decisive air nuclear attack on the USSR. . . .This could be the best time to negotiate from strength, since the U.S. military position vis-à-vis Russia might never be so strong again."[95] President Eisenhower was not convinced by the report and shelved it.[96]

During the second term of the Eisenhower administration, in contrast to the first, very little attention was paid to the vulnerabilities of the Soviet bloc. Hungary had settled that. The one area of significant change and reduced Soviet global influence was not anticipated or even recognized in U.S. policy when it became evident: the growing Sino-Soviet split. As noted earlier, intelligence estimates in the 1950s downplayed the significance of the growing strains in the relationship. Thus the basic National Intelligence Estimate on Soviet policies in late 1957 stated: "Though new points of friction will probably arise in the course of the next few years, differences will almost certainly be minor when compared to the basic points of agreement," including "ideological bonds" and also "share[d] hostility to the US."[97]

It would go beyond the present discussion to discuss other sources of Sino-Soviet estrangement, but one important element was the differing assessments in Moscow and Beijing of the American adversary and divergence over policy toward the United States. The Taiwan Straits crisis of 1958, as some U.S. analysts believed at the time, was a major source of friction. So was the growing Soviet interest in working with the United States in the field of disarmament, particularly on nuclear testing and (at that time only implicitly) nuclear nonproliferation. Khrushchev's visit to the United States in September 1959 (to be discussed presently) and his overtures for détente and disarmament

93. The Gaither Report, "Deterrence and Survival in the Nuclear Age," submitted on November 7, 1957, is in *FRUS 1955–1957* (1990), vol. 19, pp. 638–61.

94. Ibid., p. 640.

95. Ibid., p. 650.

96. The leak of the gist of the report led to a Senate debate and calls for its public release, a course supported by some of its contributors, but the president was adamant. See Morton H. Halperin, "The Gaither Committee and the Policy Process," *World Politics*, vol. 13 (April 1961), pp. 360–84.

97. NIE 11-4-57, *Main Trends in Soviet Capabilities and Policies, 1957–1962*, November 12, 1957, para. 185, p. 43.

provoked a sharp personal confrontation between Khrushchev and Mao Ze-dong when the Soviet leader stopped in Beijing on his way home from the United States (not, itself, the most tactful decision). This became a major issue between them in the international communist movement from 1960 on and in the split marked by the Soviet Union's withdrawal of its 1,300 technical advisers from China that summer.

In 1959 U.S. intelligence estimators were not sufficiently aware of the importance of "the American issue" in worsening Sino-Soviet relations. But this and other issues were raised and debated in the early 1960s in the international communist movement, and the United States and its allies became aware of them from numerous penetrations of Western and neutral Communist parties and eventually openly published diatribes. Intelligence on the developing rift from 1960 onward was quite good. There were, however, no U.S. policy changes to take advantage of this situation.

The changing strategic situation in the years 1957–60 caused a significant change in the focus of U.S. assessments of the Soviet adversary. Instead of merely refining their estimates of Soviet tactics in pursuing now-familiar objectives with improving but also familiar military capabilities, these assessments had begun to reevaluate both Soviet intentions and capabilities for the future. While the United States continued to enjoy strategic superiority, at least for a time, the key difference from the 1953–56 period was that in 1957–60 and thereafter the United States was fast losing its previous invulnerability. Mutual vulnerability brought mutual deterrence from unprovoked attack, but it eroded American ability to rely on its strategic nuclear power to deter a range of lesser provocations "at times and places of our choosing." Moreover, some even questioned whether the United States would long retain a deterrent to direct attack.

The Soviet Union was also seen as more assertive in extending its presence beyond Eurasia, possibly portending increasing communist subversion, and above all new assertiveness in Europe, with the opening wedge in Berlin. This new threat had been foreshadowed in the Suez crisis in November 1956 by Khrushchev's rocket rattling, termed "atomic blackmail" by some, which sought to divide the Western alliance by widening the breach caused by the U.S. opposition to Britain and France over Suez and by threatening other allies by bluntly drawing attention to the devastation caused by even a few nuclear missiles. But the threat took on new significance with the Soviet development of intercontinental missiles that could perhaps checkmate U.S. nuclear support for Europe. And Berlin was, in the eyes of many Europeans, an anomaly that was not worth the risk of nuclear war.

Official U.S. intelligence and related policymaking assessments in the second Eisenhower administration addressed three basic questions: the Soviet Union's aims and course of action with regard to Berlin, its long-term strategic nuclear capabilities, and its long-term objectives for exploiting its growing strategic nuclear strength. There were, of course, other developments requiring consideration, including in this new context the old issues of East-West security and disarmament, as well as others prompted by new developments in the world.

Khrushchev, in a speech in November 1958 followed by a formal diplomatic note, called for the termination of the four-power role in Berlin and the signing of a German peace treaty within six months.[98] That led to intermittent crises over the next four years. From the outset, the matter was taken as a serious challenge by the Western leaders.[99] Khrushchev subsequently tried to exploit the tension he had generated not only to get new negotiations going on Berlin and Germany, including a summit, but also to force broader negotiations.

The American intelligence and foreign policy community, both in 1958 and later, generally agreed that the Soviet Union's initiative on Berlin was an attempt to change the status quo to its advantage on the basis of increasing Soviet strategic military power. There was also a consensus that this included both offensive and defensive elements; that is, it aimed both to disrupt the West and to consolidate Soviet hegemony in the East. There were, however, two areas of disagreement in American assessments. First, although the majority saw the principal Soviet aim as an offensive threat, some analysts believed a defensive purpose was uppermost. Second, views were divided on how

---

98. Khrushchev's initial demand, in a speech on November 10, 1958, did not include the six-month deadline added in the formal note to the other three powers on November 27.

Sergo Mikoyan, son of the late Soviet Politburo member Anastas Mikoyan, has told me that Khrushchev's speech had not been discussed and cleared with the other Soviet leaders. Former First Deputy Foreign Minister Georgy Kornienko has told me that he believes the inspiration for Khrushchev's initiative stemmed from Georgy Pushkin, a senior Foreign Ministry official and former ambassador to East Germany, serving in 1958–59 as chief of an Estimates Department of the Central Committee. He states that Pushkin had drawn Khrushchev's attention to a speech by Secretary Dulles in October 1958 comparing the importance of Quemoy and Matsu with West Berlin, and that thinking about this had led Khrushchev to decide to push on Berlin!

99. For example, on the day after the speech, Ambassador Thompson in Moscow cabled Washington, calling it "a most dangerous move on the part of Khrushchev," and said "this faces us with an exceedingly dangerous situation." Ambassador Thompson, Embassy Moscow cable 1052, November 11, 1958, pp. 1, 2. The State Department's Bureau of Intelligence and Research also concluded that "the West must expect a serious increase of tensions over Berlin." Hugh S. Cumming, Jr., INR, "Khrushchev's Speech of November 10," November 12, 1958, p. 2. This was also true of allied reactions.

determined the Soviets were to press ahead unilaterally if the West stood firm on maintaining the status quo.

The president and Secretary Dulles, and most policymakers, saw the offensive threat to the West as dominant and were determined to stand fast even if armed hostilities ensued. President Eisenhower's own later account identifies the Soviet move on Berlin as a manifestation of a propensity by the communists "to make trouble wherever they saw a promising opportunity."[100] Nonetheless, in addition to the vitally important dimension of maintaining allied unity on handling the challenge to Berlin, assessments of Soviet intentions with respect to concrete actions were extremely important. The main proponents of the view that Khrushchev would follow through on his threats to challenge Western occupation rights in West Berlin and access to East Berlin and to sign a separate peace treaty with East Germany were the intelligence office and some others in the Department of State, as well as some in the Pentagon. Although there was also a range of views in the CIA, its intelligence estimators succeeded in overriding the State Department representatives who predicted that the Soviet Union would follow through on its threats. While cautiously noting uncertainties, the CIA estimators believed that Khrushchev would back down, as he repeatedly did.

The American (and Western) consensus on a firm stand did not preclude some differences on tactics, even important ones. For example, British Prime Minister Harold Macmillan in 1959 wanted a summit to deal with the issue (as did Khrushchev), but President Eisenhower resolutely rejected such a meeting "under duress," and the Paris summit of May 1960 (which aborted for other reasons) was agreed upon only after Khrushchev had withdrawn any deadline or ultimative threat. (The original six-month deadline called for on November 27, 1958, was dropped quietly; a new deadline imposed on June 10, 1959, was dropped by Khrushchev at Camp David on September 27, 1959.) Nonetheless, the American and allied consensus held up. The Berlin and German issue was ultimately left pending for the succeeding U.S. administration in 1961.

The full purpose of Khrushchev's major push on Berlin from 1958 on is not clear to this day. Many in the American leadership, including President Eisenhower at least at times, saw the Berlin challenge as ushering in two or three decades of tension as the Soviet Union pressed to take advantage of the parity

---

100. Dwight D. Eisenhower, *Waging Peace: 1956–1961* (Doubleday, 1965), p. 330. Reflecting the preoccupation of policymakers at the time, the entire chapter devoted to the Berlin crisis from November 1958 through May 1959 has no further discussion of Soviet motivations, but only of possible Soviet moves and Western countermeasures.

in strategic vulnerability and later parity in strategic forces. Some, not including the president, believed the Soviet Union was driving for and could attain a strategic superiority that would encourage and permit much stronger Soviet pressures on the West. Although the United States no longer entertained comparable counterpressures on "the Sino-Soviet bloc," such thinking did reinforce an adamant Western stand.

Some intelligence and other analysts, on the other hand, believed that Khrushchev, while trying to cash in on an improved Soviet strategic position, was primarily seeking to consolidate the Soviet position in Eastern Europe (to get rid of this "bone in his throat," as he colorfully put it), gain Western acceptance of the division of Germany, and if possible head off the full integration of the Federal Republic of Germany into NATO. (In precisely these years, the United States moved forward with plans, known to Soviet intelligence in 1958 and public by 1960, for arming the Bundeswehr with nuclear weapons, albeit under American custody. In 1957–58, the United States had rejected the Soviet-sponsored Rapacki Plan for military disengagement.) These analysts believed that Khrushchev sought to stabilize, rather than upset, the division of Europe, perhaps as a basis for seeking improved relations. This was also the view of Ambassador Llewellyn Thompson in Moscow.[101]

Intelligence assessments tended to embrace both offensive and defensive objectives by referring to a probable range of minimum and maximum Soviet goals, defensive ones tending to be the minimum, and offensive ones elastic to range from modest to major gains. Whatever the precise or elastic Soviet objectives, all agreed that Khrushchev was engaged in a test of Western resolve that must be met. The fact that Khrushchev sought to modulate his stand by

---

101. Ambassador Tommy Thompson in March 1959 submitted a powerful argument for the defensive nature of the Soviet stand on Berlin and for recognizing a Soviet interest in improving relations based on the status quo in Europe and in longer-term coexistence and an end to the cold war. While advanced as explaining the Soviet self-perception of its aims, and accompanied by Thompson's own reaffirmation that "we must at any cost stand by our commitment to West Berlin," this attempt to assess the Soviet motivation in defensive terms won no vocal supporters, and Thompson's own standing in the eyes of many in the administration suffered. In retrospect, it reads quite well, and the late ambassador deserves recognition for courageously taking an unpopular but sound stand. There was also some support for this view in the analytical Soviet affairs community (including the present author), with some reflection in the National Intelligence Estimates. But apart from Thompson, no one clearly advocated this point of view, and it did not noticeably affect policymakers. Thompson also argued, in a dissent from the then-standard line, that détente would on balance be in the U.S. interest. See Ambassador Thompson, Embassy Moscow cable 1773 to the Secretary of State, March 9, 1959, esp. pt. 2, pp. 3–4, and pt. 3, p. 4, on détente; Secret, declassified December 11, 1989, and probably to appear in a forthcoming volume of *FRUS 1958–1960*.

alternating between harsh, ultimative stands and peace proposals and calls for negotiation did not mitigate this Western assessment. On the contrary, whatever real Soviet interest there was in compelling the West to enter into broader negotiations, including talks in the field of European security and disarmament, it was undermined by its association with a policy of pressure. Similarly and more generally, Khrushchev's bluster and claims of growing missile strength and of a decisive shift in the correlation of forces ("we will bury you") undercut and precluded any real negotiations for the relaxation of tension, mutual accommodation, and disarmament.

If Khrushchev was in fact trying to force the West into détente once Berlin had been dealt with and the bloc shored up, both his policy and tactics were a major miscalculation. Whatever Khrushchev's aims, his generation of the Berlin crisis was a serious mistake. It did not stabilize the situation in Eastern Europe (only the Wall in August 1961 staunched the outflow of East Germans); it did not divide and weaken the West; it did not stop German rearmament; it did not usher in real negotiations or still less détente. On the contrary, it precluded any possibility of more favorable relations with the West during these years and burdened the prospect later; it strengthened both Western resolve and capabilities; and it was perceived to confirm Soviet hostility and a Soviet threat.

Notwithstanding the Berlin confrontation, there were, to be sure, modest steps in developing relations. But whatever potential they had for relaxing tensions and improving relations was circumscribed and even prejudiced by the recurrent Soviet pressure on the status quo in Berlin.

Personal contacts between senior leaders of the two countries were inhibited by the Berlin crisis but did nonetheless develop in periods of lesser tension during 1959.[102] Two Soviet leaders close to Khrushchev, First Deputy Prime Ministers Anastas Mikoyan and Frol Kozlov, visited the United States in January and July 1959, respectively, as precursors to a possible bilateral summit.

Mikoyan's visit provided an opportunity to try to persuade the American leaders that the Soviet aim in stirring up the Berlin issue was not to raise tensions but to remove a source of tension. When he saw the president, he

---

102. An important change in the U.S. leadership came when John Foster Dulles, hospitalized with terminal cancer, resigned in April (and died in May) 1959. He was succeeded by Christian Herter. President Eisenhower, in his letter regretfully accepting Dulles's resignation, paid him what for both was a strong compliment by stating: "You have been a staunch bulwark of our nation against the machinations of Imperialistic Communism." Cited in Eisenhower, *Waging Peace*, p. 358.

proposed that the two sides should "end the cold war."[103] He advised Secretary Dulles in advance of the Soviet public presentation of a draft peace treaty for Germany on January 10 and conspicuously did not refer to the earlier announced six-month deadline. Nonetheless, during Mikoyan's visit Dulles told a group of congressional leaders that the Soviet leader was visiting to "'spy us out' and to learn whether we were strong and unified" in standing up on Berlin.[104] While perhaps this was said to encourage bipartisan support, the remark also reflected an important element of the administration's thinking about the situation.

Vice President Richard Nixon in return (July 23 to August 2) made the highest-level U.S. visit to the Soviet Union ever (if one sets aside President Franklin Roosevelt's secret wartime meeting with Stalin at Yalta in 1945).[105] He was well received by the Soviet public, as was the first major U.S. national exhibition, which he opened; it was a great success during the whole summer.

Most significant, of course, was the visit to the United States in September by Nikita Khrushchev. President Eisenhower's return visit was scheduled for June 1960.[106] The Kozlov and Nixon visits developed contact, but were not used to advance the discussion of policy issues. The only direct policy link in this chain was a broken one. The invitation for Khrushchev to come to the United States was extended by Under Secretary of State Robert Murphy (through Kozlov, on July 12) without reference to an important intended precondition. Murphy did not understand and convey that the invitation was conditioned on progress in a forthcoming Geneva meeting of the foreign ministers on Berlin. The error was discovered only after Khrushchev had accepted the unconditioned invitation.[107]

The climax of summit diplomacy in the Eisenhower years, as noted above, came with Khrushchev's visit to the United States and the meetings at Camp David. The only concrete accomplishment was the defusing of the Berlin crisis sufficient to permit agreement on a multilateral summit in Paris the next May, but the establishment of somewhat better personal rapport (and the opportunity for Khrushchev to see something of the United States in a twelve-day visit)

103. Memorandum of Conversation, "Mikoyan's Call on the President," January 17, 1959 (drafted by Ambassador Thompson; Secret, declassified March 10, 1989), p. 6.

104. "Bipartisan Congressional Meeting," White House Transcript, January 5, 1959.

105. I accompanied the vice president as his CIA adviser on the trip.

106. I participated in planning this trip, as I had the Nixon visit, and was scheduled also to accompany the president.

107. See Eisenhower, *Waging Peace*, pp. 405–08.

were also useful. So, too, in my judgment, would have been the planned week-long visit of President Eisenhower to the Soviet Union (which was to include a trip across Siberia and departure via the Pacific).

It remains an open question whether the planned summit in Paris, had it not been aborted by the shooting down of an intruding American U-2 deep over Soviet territory on May 1, 1960, would have led to any constructive result or would have failed.[108] In the event, the U-2 incident not only canceled the Paris summit and President Eisenhower's visit to the USSR, but essentially froze Soviet-U.S. relations until a new American administration came into office. And then relations were activated but rapidly deteriorated through the Vienna summit of June 1961 into the most intense stage of the Berlin crisis from June to October of that year, and to the Cuban missile crisis of October 1962.

The U-2 incident of May 1960 deserves attention for another reason. It was a most unfortunate episode. Inescapably, the United States bore responsibility for the flight and hence for the consequences. Nor can one blame the Soviet Union for shooting down the plane. Nonetheless, in a broad sense it would certainly have been in the interest of both countries if the plane had not been shot down. By the same token, one may of course say that the flight should not have been permitted. It is, however, necessary to consider why President Eisenhower authorized that (and earlier) flights, contravening international law and with an inherent risk of considerable diplomatic cost. Although the program of U-2 reconnaissance penetrations of the Soviet Union did not prevent the issue of a missile gap from arising, it did help keep U.S. estimates of Soviet missile advances from getting out of hand. The fateful mission of May 1, had it not been lost, would have made a major contribution to laying to rest the charges and fears of a missile gap that, in turn, worked against an improvement in U.S.-Soviet relations and stimulated U.S. military programs that heated up the arms race.[109] In that sense, the biggest cost of the incident was that it postponed for a crucial year or so (and with a change of American leadership) the dispelling of the missile gap fears in the United States.

It is sometimes said that President Eisenhower knew there was no missile gap because of the U-2. That is partly true. Eisenhower was confident that there

108. The most comprehensive account is Michael R. Beschloss, *Mayday: Eisenhower, Khrushchev and the U-2 Affair* (Harper and Row, 1986).

109. I vividly recall how, as a senior intelligence analyst and estimates officer, I and my colleagues were awaiting the results of that flight, which would have confirmed the four launchers at the only operational Soviet ICBM site (at Plesetsk) and negated several other suspect sites, and my shocked disappointment when a colleague came into my office that day and

was no impending missile gap because of his reading of the available evidence (from the U-2 photography and other sources) and feel for the Soviet Union. Many of us in the intelligence-estimating business held that same view. But we could not persuade others in the estimates process, nor could the president persuade skeptics, because the evidence was indicative and substantial, but not conclusive. Available evidence was not sufficient to rule out other possibilities. Although those who advanced more dire estimates of existing (and especially future) Soviet missile capabilities could not, of course, prove their case, it could not then be completely disproved.

The drama leading up to and following from the shooting down of the U-2 illustrates a number of the difficulties in assessment and policymaking within and between the two governments.

President Eisenhower did not realize that his resumption of penetrating U-2 flights on April 9 and May 1, 1960—the first ones after Camp David—had put Khrushchev on the spot in a politically vulnerable position for his policy of détente with the United States (including the added strains on Sino-Soviet relations). Khrushchev, in turn, did not realize how much Eisenhower needed the information from the U-2 flights to keep at bay the pressures for a crash U.S. military buildup. After the shooting down, Khrushchev did not realize that by publicly taunting Eisenhower with the idea that any U.S. general could start a war he was forcing the president to assume responsibility. Eisenhower (and others in Washington) did not pick up on Ambassador Thompson's suggestion that Khrushchev was trying to find a way out and resume his détente policy, but it is hard to see how the outcome could have been avoided by that time. The president did not seek any intelligence assessment of Soviet policy or political

said simply, "It's down." "Where?" I asked. "Sverdlovsk." I suddenly recalled my own sighting of two SA-2 air-defense missile launch complexes near Sverdlovsk the previous July when I accompanied Nixon, and wondered if I had seen the unit that shot down the U-2. Only years later did I find confirmation from the memoir of one of Gary Powers's Soviet military interrogators that it had indeed been the air-defense complex at Kosulino, thirty-two kilometers southeast of Sverdlovsk, which I had observed as we flew into Sverdlovsk, that shot down Powers's U-2. See Lt. General of Justice N. F. Chistyakov, *Po zakonu i sovesti* (By law and conscience) (Moscow: Voyenizdat [Military publishing house], 1979), p. 144.

It had been reported at the time, incorrectly, that Nixon himself had seen a new type of air-defense complex near Sverdlovsk. *Aviation Week*, May 16, 1960; cited by David Wise and Thomas B. Ross, *The U-2 Affair* (Random House, 1962), p. 27; and Beschloss, *Mayday*, pp. 182–83. This was a garbled leak of the sighting I had made while a member of the vice president's delegation.

On Plesetsk as the chief target of the U-2 flight, and only operational ICBM site, see among other published sources Beschloss, *Mayday*, pp. 241–42, 341.

ramifications; the overwhelming concern of the White House was naturally focused on U.S. (and presidential) political standing at home and in the world, not on pulling Khrushchev's chestnuts out of the fire.

There was no basis for confidential exchanges even if either leader had been disposed to use them. There were no back-channel intermediaries of the kind that Kennedy and Nixon later had, for possible exploration of ways out of the dilemma.

The U-2 affair marked the beginning of Khrushchev's decline and ultimate fall from power and, as far as U.S.-Soviet relations were concerned, the end of the Eisenhower presidency.[110] It left, of course, the issues of the military balance and the unresolved political confrontation over Berlin.

From 1957 until 1961, U.S. uncertainties about Soviet ICBM capabilities paralleled uncertainties about the calculation underlying their political offensive on Berlin. Did the Soviet leaders know something we did not about their emerging capabilities? Clearly they did, but it was not, as many in Washington then feared, that they were moving forward more rapidly; it was in fact a deception to conceal their weakness, and, to the extent their political drive rested on it, a bluff. Despite uncertainties and divided judgments in Washington on Soviet capabilities, the bluff failed because there was determination not to yield even—or especially—if the capabilities threat was in fact growing rapidly.

The overall U.S. assessment of Soviet intentions as well as capabilities was heavily influenced by the conjunction of the missile claims and political demands on Berlin. Until informed Soviet evaluations can clarify the Soviet actions of the period, it would appear that although Khrushchev's personal style of conducting policy was an added irritant, any Soviet leadership would have sought to stabilize the situation in Europe. Would a different leadership also have had less inclination to try to benefit from the emerging strategic parity? Would it have chosen to concentrate on Berlin? A second and related critical question is whether different Soviet diplomatic approaches would have been met by different American responses.

Other aspects of the development of U.S.-Soviet relations in these years offer little clue. There was an incipient opening up of travel in the Soviet Union in 1957,

---

110. Years later Khrushchev confided to his American physician, "From the time Gary Powers was shot down in a U-2 over the Soviet Union I was no longer in full control." See Dr. A. McGhee Harvey, "A 1969 Conversation with Khrushchev: The Beginning of His Fall from Power," *Life*, December 18, 1970, p. 488.

and a first cultural exchange agreement with the United States in 1958.[111] In multilateral forums, although Eisenhower's Atoms for Peace proposal did not succeed in its broader aims—nor did initiatives on both sides for a curb on nuclear testing—the International Atomic Energy Agency was created in 1957 with Soviet as well as U.S. support. A multilateral treaty on Antarctica (including arms control constraints) was signed in 1959.[112]

Disarmament was a subject of interest to both President Eisenhower and Khrushchev. Yet no agreements were reached, for a number of reasons: the intractability of the problems, opposition from powerful institutional interests in both countries, the lack of sufficient reciprocal confidence, and the uncertainties and blank spots in intelligence. The absence of adequate information on key military developments, compounded by Soviet objections to intrusive verification, severely limited the possibilities. So did the assessment of Soviet political and military objectives by U.S. leaders, as earlier discussed, and probably also the Soviet assessment of U.S. and NATO political and military objectives.

Yet there was little appreciation of these factors, particularly the interactive ones. Neither side had more than scratched the surface when it came to empathetic understanding of the perspective or perceptions of the other side.

Some modest efforts in this direction were made. For example, an assessment of Soviet disarmament motivations is instructive. While Soviet positions on particular disarmament issues had of course been addressed in various intelligence estimates, a Special National Intelligence Estimate entitled "The

111. In March 1958 Eisenhower was inclined to propose an exchange to bring 10,000 Soviet students to American universities, but Dulles talked him out of it. See William Bragg Ewald, Jr., *Eisenhower the President, Crucial Days, 1951–1960* (Prentice-Hall, 1981), pp. 213–16.

112. In preparation for possible negotiations on Antarctica, a Special National Intelligence Estimate (SNIE 11-3-58), *Soviet Reactions to Possible United States Actions on Antarctica*, was prepared in early 1958; issued February 11, 1958; Secret, now declassified. I was the drafting officer. It was estimated that the Soviet Union would probably attend if the United States called for such a conference, and would probably join if its access and status protected its interests. While unexceptional, and validated by events, at the time there were those who doubted Soviet readiness for any cooperative venture. The estimate reinforced the positions favored by Secretary of State Dulles (and probably President Eisenhower) on two issues where there were opposing views within the administration: on whether to assert formal U.S. claims (which the JCS favored), and on whether to invite the USSR to an international conference (which the JCS and a number of other senior officials were doubtful about or opposed). The role of this national estimate was therefore passive, but a contrary judgment in the SNIE could have had a significant impact. The key NSC meeting for which the SNIE had been prepared was held on March 6, 1958. U.S. policy papers on Antarctica for the years 1955–60 are in *FRUS 1955–1957* (1988), vol. 11,

Soviet Attitude toward Disarmament" was undertaken in 1958.[113] By then the Soviet leaders had proposed a wide range of arms control initiatives including a nuclear test moratorium, a nuclear-free zone in Central Europe, and troop reductions in Europe. The estimate addressed positive motivations and restraining considerations in Soviet policymaking on disarmament, as well as concrete issues.

The estimate credited the Soviet leadership with genuine security concerns and a desire to reduce the risks of nuclear war, coupled with a growing confidence and belief that a positive stance would promote their "strategy of peaceful competition." Moreover, with the coming of mutual deterrence, "they might see considerable value in entering negotiations with respect to the stabilization of the nuclear balance of power at a certain level."[114] This forecast was substantiated a decade later in the SALT negotiations.

The SNIE also noted several restraining elements in Soviet policymaking, and "powerfully reinforcing this attitude of caution is a deeply ingrained suspicion of the disarmament position taken by the West."[115] On balance, it concluded, "To date Soviet disarmament policy seems dominated by such an attitude of caution, by acute suspicion of Western motives, and by the feeling that the vulnerability of the Western position can continue to be exploited at minimum cost to the Soviets themselves."[116] Although it did not rule out serious negotiations, the intelligence estimate concluded that "the Soviets probably believe that the West is not yet ready to agree to arms limitations on any basis which seems equitable to the USSR. They see the U.S. as not yet having reconciled itself to the Bloc's enhanced power position. . . . For their own part, believing that time is working in their favor, they may see advantages in postponing serious negotiations . . . until their position is further strengthened, especially through the advent of a substantial ICBM capability."[117] Nonetheless, for the longer term the prospect was judged more favorably:

---

pp. 607–722, and *FRUS 1958–1960* (1991), vol. 2, pp. 464–640. SNIE 11-3-58 was not declassified in time for inclusion in *FRUS*.

The Treaty on Antarctica contained a number of unprecedented arms control restrictions, including effective demilitarization, cooperative inspection for verification, and measures creating the world's first nuclear-free zone.

113. SNIE 11-6-58, *The Soviet Attitude toward Disarmament*, June 24, 1958; Secret, declassified with minor deletions. I was the principal drafter of the estimate.

114. Ibid., para. 19, p. 5.

115. Ibid., para. 26, p. 6.

116. Ibid., para. 31, p. 7.

117. Ibid., para. 32, p. 8.

"both foreign policy and security motivations may lead to growing Soviet interest in expanding the areas of serious disarmament negotiations."[118]

The special estimate on disarmament, as well as other estimates of military policy, found a conservative majority view and a very hard minority position on the projection of Soviet military programs. The estimate stated that "their basic view of Western hostility will impel the Soviet leaders to retain at least sufficient military deterrent power to meet what they regard as minimum deterrent needs." It concluded, however, that "the USSR will enter any disarmament agreement with the intent at the same time to seek constantly to enhance its military capabilities and to achieve an eventual military superiority over the U.S."[119] This estimate was offset, to a degree, by the further judgment that "we do not believe they can realistically count on being able to achieve a decisive superiority in overall strategic delivery capability," which provoked a formal Air Force dissent.[120]

Estimates of Soviet military forces, and especially of anticipated future force developments, during the period from 1955 to 1961 reflected sharply divided views. From 1955 to 1958, a bomber gap projecting a major buildup in the Soviet bomber force fueled fears of Soviet military power as well as a stepped-up U.S. Air Force bomber buildup. The Soviet bomber buildup never occurred, and by 1958 projected Soviet heavy bomber levels were cut by 80 percent.[121] The famous missile gap of 1958–61 followed. Again, projections of a Soviet ICBM buildup were grossly exaggerated, including the initial deployments and the projected buildup.[122] It was not until shortly after the end of the

118. Ibid., para. 5, p. 2.

119. Ibid., para. 6, p. 2; as is evident, the language bridged two different views of Soviet military policy aims.

120. Ibid., para. 18, p. 5. The Air Force intelligence chief believed the overall tenor of the estimate "suggests a Soviet willingness to curtail or limit the development of their capabilities to a level of deterrence rather than to seek the early attainment of an overpowering military superiority," and wanted the estimate to say that any Soviet disarmament agreement would be entered into with the intention of "furthering their drive toward world domination," and would "in no way lead them to lessen their efforts to achieve an overpowering nuclear delivery capability at the earliest possible time." Ibid., pp. 2, 5, footnotes of dissent by the Assistant Chief of Staff, Intelligence, U.S. Air Force.

121. See John Prados, *The Soviet Estimate: U.S. Intelligence Analysis and Russian Military Strength* (Dial Press, 1982), pp. 38–50; and Lawrence Freedman, *U.S. Intelligence and the Soviet Strategic Threat* (Westview Press, 1977), pp. 65–67.

122. See Prados, *Soviet Estimate*, pp. 67–95, 111–26; and Freedman, *U.S. Intelligence*, pp. 67–80.

Eisenhower administration that the missile gap could be put to rest, and it was exploited effectively by the Democrats in the 1960 election.[123]

President Eisenhower himself was skeptical of such Soviet prowess and military buildup and was persuaded by the intelligence. But, as noted earlier, the evidence was not sufficient to dispel the alarmist views, fed by the Air Force and such studies as the Gaither Report.

The assessment of Soviet conventional forces was not attended by comparable alarm and controversy. A Special National Intelligence Estimate in early 1960, sparked by Khrushchev's revelation of the size of the Soviet armed forces and his announced further reductions (beyond earlier ones of 1955–58), started the estimates on a path of increasing precision and downgrading of earlier, somewhat inflated estimates as more evidence was acquired.[124]

The military estimates became increasingly accurate, but Soviet strategic military power was increasing—not, as some feared, toward superiority over the United States, but eroding the superiority to which the United States had become accustomed. President Eisenhower was convinced that his military programs met U.S. security requirements. It is clear in retrospect that they did, but that was not evident to many Americans in 1960. Nor were the limits to Soviet ambitions and potential pressures, as on Berlin, or prospects for mischief making in the third world. The Sino-Soviet rift, while remarkable, did not lead to a reassessment of the relevance of communist ideology as a force in world politics.

The Eisenhower administration thus left office in 1961 with many accomplishments, but also with the Republican candidate defeated at the polls and under fire for alleged weakness in building military capabilities (the missile gap) and in demonstrating political resolution (in particular over Cuba in the

---

123. I had informally given a talk to a Democratic Senate Study Group in 1960, at which the subject of the missile gap came up. Senator Stuart Symington was among those present, and he followed up with me later although without being persuaded. I could not, of course, use special intelligence in talking with him. Allen Dulles was properly wary of such extracurricular activities, but did not forbid it. My position was that there was no prospective gap, which was also the administration's stand in opposition to the Democratic criticisms.

124. SNIE 11-6-60, *Strength of the Armed Forces of the USSR,* May 3, 1960; Secret, declassified September 9, 1981. I drafted this estimate, and I have described the process in "Estimating Soviet Military Force Levels: Some Light from the Past," *International Security,* vol. 14 (Spring 1990), pp. 93–116, which also appends the full text of the SNIE. After this estimate was prepared and accepted by the intelligence community, Director Allen Dulles told me, in a bizarre compliment, "Ray, you've gotten rid of more Soviet divisions than anyone since Hitler!"

Kennedy-Nixon debate). This was unfair and unjust—as had been the charges of Democratic weakness in 1952.

The interrelationships between personalized intuitive and formalized analytical assessments are richly reflected in the experience of the evaluations of the Soviet adversary by the Eisenhower administration. So, too, are the interrelationships between the assessments of intentions (both long-term goals and short-term policy objectives) and capabilities (both actual operative and potential assets and projected future acquisitions). The domestic political climate and the international environment both impinge on the conduct of U.S.-Soviet relations (and, of course, on Soviet-U.S. relations) and on perceptions of the adversary. The impact of interrelationships between the two sides—often failures to connect—was also important.

The historical continuities loom large, notwithstanding changes—even important changes—within a system of views. American concerns over the predicated ultimate aims of communist world domination and perceptions of more proximate Soviet objectives, policies, and actions seen as threatening to American interests persisted from the Truman administration at least through that of President Ronald Reagan, enjoying a renaissance in the early 1980s. Only now is that changing as the Soviet Union for all practical purposes is abandoning communism, as it has already released the former communist bloc. The Eisenhower administration and its successors adopted an inherited U.S. anticommunist and anti-Soviet policy of containment.

During the Eisenhower administration (coinciding with the post-Stalin period in the Soviet Union), the consensus was that there was no imminent threat of war and, although not explicitly so articulated, also that war was not inevitable. That was the crucial foundation for the rejection of preventive war, taken for granted now but not at the time that the Eisenhower administration entered office.

There was also a persistent tendency dating from NSC 68 and the impact of the Korean War and continuing through the Eisenhower years, and intermittently on through the first Reagan administration, to overestimate both future Soviet military capabilities and future Soviet political aggressiveness. To his great credit, President Eisenhower himself had a much more realistic assessment on both counts and helped restrain the alarmism stimulated by such developments as the scare caused by Sputnik and the fears of an ICBM missile gap. But in retrospect it is clear that even he and his administration—like both the predecessor and successor Democratic administrations—greatly overstated to themselves the real Soviet threat. This included a much exaggerated image of the capacity of the Soviet leadership and "world communism" to pose a subversive threat to the rest of the world. The corrosive effect of this acceptance and inversion of the communist ideological conception of a struggle of two worlds led, among other mistaken assessments, to an aggregation of the rest of the world, despite its diversities, into the "free world." It also harnessed U.S. objectives into excessively single-minded priorities on accepting and building anticommunist regimes without sufficient attention to other American, and global, interests.

Another effect of the American assessment of an imposed zero-sum contest was the conclusion that the United States, too, must play the game of political, economic, and covert warfare. Some results were undoubtedly constructive, on their own merits as well as for their cold war purposes. The Marshall Plan is foremost. To cite but one much less obvious example, the covert CIA programs funding and supporting a host of liberal causes (such as the Congress of Cultural Freedom and *Encounter* and *Der Monat* magazines) stimulated intellectual development.

Not all American covert activities were similarly constructive. Today there are conflicting judgments on the merits of even superficially successful actions such as the overthrow of Mossadeq in Iran and Arbenz in Guatemala. And there are yet undivulged cases, on both sides, of successful disinformation campaigns that may have had many innocent victims, such as the reported CIA role (before the Eisenhower administration) in instigating the Noel Field case and its enormous ripple effects in purging many early postwar communist leaders in several countries of Eastern Europe and thousands of their supporters.[125] It certainly created disarray in the communist world. Other covert intelligence operations, such as disinformation designed to mislead the adversary on U.S.

---

125. I cite this case because it has recently surfaced in the Soviet Union, as well as earlier in the West. In brief, Noel Field, despite extensive communist ties, had served in the wartime Office of Strategic Services (OSS) under Allen Dulles under cover of the Unitarian Service Committee. He had used that position to aid a number of Central and East European communist leaders to escape to the West. In 1949, Josef Swiatlo, a senior Polish security police officer (and CIA agent), drew attention to Fields's OSS connections, leading to Fields's arrest in Prague. Among Fields's wartime communist connections who then became purge victims were Rudolf Slansky in Czechoslovakia and Laszlo Rajk in Hungary. Swiatlo, who later escaped to the West, has affirmed this account. It has not been confirmed by U.S. or Soviet intelligence. See Alexander Potekhin, "Secret Services: Betrayed by Dulles and Beria," *New Times*, no. 33 (August 1990), pp. 34–36 (interestingly, this article did not appear in the Russian-language edition of the journal, *Novoye vremya*). See also Stewart Steven, *Operation Splinter Factor* (J. B. Lippincott, 1974).

military programs, may have contributed to the wasteful Soviet diversion of resources, but at a cost of heightening suspicion and contributing to a more open-ended arms competition.

With the exception of such intelligence disinformation, intelligence information collection should be distinguished from covert operations intended to act on the opponent. Intelligence is, after all, a critical necessary element in policy formation.

The importance of blanks and uncertainties with respect to Soviet military capabilities and Soviet political intentions in affecting U.S. assessments has not been adequately recognized. Although the errors in overestimating military capabilities tended to be recognized after time (and after building American forces), errors in political assessment not only have not been similarly validated but in many cases remain uncertain to this day. Were there real possibilities for major accomplishments concerning Germany and European security in the mid-1950s? Had there been another "opening" in 1959–63, as Ambassador Anatoly Dobrynin (in that period, chief of the American Department in the Soviet Foreign Ministry) later told Henry Kissinger?[126] Was Khrushchev's persistent pressure on Berlin for four years an excessively blustering attempt to clear the decks for détente, or, if successful, was it merely the first of a series of escalating demands? Were there unrealized possibilities for arms control and disarmament? (On a nuclear test ban, almost certainly yes; on strategic arms limitations, almost certainly no, given the disparities in forces at that time.)

Another often unappreciated result of the uncertainties and blank spots, apart from conservative assessments to compensate, is the stimulus for more intelligence. The classic case was the highly successful U-2 intelligence collection program and its ultimately disastrous diplomatic consequence. The quest for intelligence information often burdens, if it does not undercut, diplomatic efforts to reduce tensions. Yet it is necessary not only for defense, but for reasoned initiatives for improving relations.

Intelligence assessment became more refined and sophisticated during the Eisenhower years, although there were limits not only to its capabilities but also to receptivity by those engaged in the policy process. For anyone other than the president himself (excepting perhaps Secretary Dulles or CIA Director Dulles in private conversations), there were restraints against suggestions as to Soviet policy motivation that departed from the implicit stereotypical cold war

126. Henry Kissinger, *White House Years* (Little, Brown, 1979), p. 113.

consensus. Although this did not prevent George Kennan, Chip Bohlen, or Tommy Thompson from making their views known, it did affect their careers and influence—to say nothing of the indirect effect on others of less established stature. Nonetheless, McCarthyism was virtually absent from the intelligence community, and the greatest leeway for "new thinking" in the Eisenhower years was to be found in the CIA, in the Intelligence Directorate and especially in the Office of National Estimates.[127] Not only were liberals and Democrats welcome—if they were keen analysts—but so were insightful analyses, even if they challenged established views.

It is difficult, from the documentary record even supplemented by personal observation and experience from participation, to judge the real impact of intelligence assessment on policymaking. Certainly the bureaucratically organized process of the work of the NSC machinery in the Eisenhower administration—never equaled since—had negative as well as positive qualities, as some of us saw at the time and many have criticized since. But there were also virtues, one of which was an integration of intelligence assessment and policy planning and decision.

The principal fault of the process of assessing the adversary, in the Eisenhower years but equally in most other administrations, was the inability to empathize with the other side and visualize its interests in other than adversarial terms. For example, it has been rare to see assessments at any time (at least before the 1990s) ascribe the prosperity, well-being, and progress of the Soviet peoples as interests of Soviet leaders. Interests in Soviet security, as opposed to aggrandizement, were recognized and noted in National Intelligence Estimates, despite carping and occasional written dissents from some in the military intelligence agencies. But there was never adequate recognition in American assessments of the need to weigh Soviet threat assessments and concerns over *our* military buildup activities and alliance building and global basing, for example, to say nothing of our covert operations in Eastern Europe and even in the USSR, overflights, covert penetrations of coastal waters, and the like.

The Eisenhower administration carried forward the national consensus on a policy of waging the cold war, seen as forced upon us by Soviet communist hostility and aggressive pursuit of world domination. Within that established

127. Although there were many variations and some clear exceptions, views in the Clandestine Services—covert action, espionage, and above all counterintelligence—ended to be very hard-line. This had, however, virtually no impact on the assessment process owing to the self-imposed isolation of the clandestine operators, not only within the government but within the CIA itself.

framework, assessment of the adversary was realistic and, given the limitations on available information, generally sound. In a broader sense, again within the constraints of the cold war worldview, it assessed developments around the world reasonably well. In particular, President Eisenhower helped to keep both assessments and policy within reasonable bounds. Above all, he steered the United States through a transition from strategic invulnerability to mutual deterrence based on mutual vulnerability, a qualitative change that was even more important than the transition from quantitative U.S. superiority to parity in strategic forces a decade or more later under President Nixon.

The American policy of containment pursued throughout the Eisenhower administration succeeded. Nonetheless, a more measured and realistic assessment of the threat, of both Soviet intentions and capabilities, might have contributed to an equally or more successful outcome at less cost to other American interests, less later risk, and perhaps a less extended period of the cold war. Too much depends upon the interaction with Soviet assessments and policy choices to be certain of that judgment, but it deserves further consideration.

Too little attention has been paid in strategic studies, diplomatic history, and intelligence analysis to the subject of assessing the adversary. More needs to be done in the United States, a start needs to be made in the Soviet Union, and eventually a process of joint analysis could be most useful of all.